THE
NEW SOCIAL
CONTRACT

RENEWING THE LIBERAL VISION
FOR AUSTRALIA

TIM WILSON

CONNOR COURT PUBLISHING PTY LTD
PO Box 7257
Redland Bay QLD 4165
online@connorcourt.com

www.connorcourtpublishing.com.au

ISBN: 978-1-922449-03-0 (pbk.)

Cover design by Ian James

Printed in Australia

PRAISE FOR *THE NEW SOCIAL CONTRACT*

"From Menzies's 'forgotten people' and the 'Howard battlers' to today's 'quiet Australians', the Liberal Party has always sought to represent the breadth of aspiration in Australian life. We do this as Liberals through what John Howard celebrated as our broad church bringing together classic liberal and conservative traditions. Tim Wilson challenges us to reflect on the philosophical timbers that build modern Australia and to see how liberalism might be shaped in the 2020s. This book prods, stirs and challenges us but ultimately asks us to think about how we will leave future generations of Australians a country that is prosperous, fairer, and where the bonds between us all are strengthened."

SCOTT MORRISON MP

Prime Minister of Australia

"Wilson is a well-read clear thinker who understands the foundations of Australian liberalism. He junks 'popcorn politics' for the real issues that advance individual empowerment, liberal justice, and an ownership society."

AMANDA VANSTONE AO

Former Howard Government minister

"Tim Wilson has always been a fearless and passionate advocate for liberalism within Australian politics, society, and economy. He has now offered a testament of that faith in *The New Social Contract* which is informative and instructive, reasoned but provocative, contemporary yet draws on classical philosophy. It should serve as a rallying call for the revival of liberalism. And it is a book that every modern Liberal should read."

TROY BRAMSTON

Author of *Robert Menzies: The Art of Politics*

"Thanks to *The New Social Contract*, I know what liberals should fight for in the 2020s. Good on Tim Wilson for putting in the thought, time and effort to move us on from popcorn politics. It's a top read providing a deeper sense of what it means to be liberal and have a better handle on where liberals need to go. It's rare to see deep conviction, thought and the pen in action. Intergenerational justice, the power of our federation and the need for us to think big and contemplate what needs to be done for betterment gave me great energy and excitement for Australia's liberal future."

RUSSEL HOWCROFT

Contents

Acknowledgements

As our whole is the greater of the sum of our parts there are some people whose contribution to this book deserves thanks for aiding me in turning keystrokes into something more substantial.

One of the most disturbing discoveries in writing a book on Australian liberalism is essentially how little has been written in Australia. There is too much reliance on foreign perspectives. Therefore, my thanks go to Professor Greg Craven, the PM Glynn Institute and the Australian Catholic University for supporting this project. It is the rumination of concerns and observations about the society and economy we live in today. The resolution of some problems only creates and exacerbates new ones. Consideration of their consequences, and what to do about them, is part of the compounding knowledge to contribute to human progress, even if it is primarily so people can say it is wrong. So their toleration of the views I proffer from an 'out' non-believer, cultural Anglican perspective comes with my thanks.

My greatest appreciation is to my editor, Damien Freeman. Parliamentarians' lives are busy without adding the writing of a book on top. He encouraged me to write. He also encouraged me to set and meet deadlines. They were definitely set. So I appreciate his patience for the latter. I've concluded that half of the role of an editor is knowing deadlines will not be met, and therefore managing their own expectations with unrepentant pressure on the author to focus their mind and fingers. His feedback and counsel was wise and his knowledge of eighteenth and nineteenth-century history superb. He would have made an outstanding Lord of Lindfield in Wentworth's bunyip aristocracy, only to be cruelly denied his birthright by liberals like me.

To two people who have shaped my understanding of liberalism. First, Dr David Kemp, whose writings have become the authoritative works on Australian liberal history and are heavily referenced in these pages, and who is always available for a liberalism counselling session as required. Secondly, to John Roskam, who has always backed me and is fearless in testing the spectrum of ideas about 'liberalisms' in public debate. We need more courageous contrarians.

To Shaun Levin and Cathy Baker, who saw in me some kernel of talent in my late twenties and have been part of my support act ever since, as our relationship easily vacillates between professional and personal with the aid of occasional alcoholic lubrication.

Finally, thanks must go to my husband, Ryan Bolger, for his endless sacrifice to support me. So the old saying goes in politics—politicians are the volunteers, families are conscripts. But Ryan married me knowing what he was getting himself into. He's sometimes a reluctant volunteer, but one none-the-same. Like all projects, he's supported me in this one even though his 2019/2020 summer was interrupted by the gnashing of keys and the spread of books and papers all over our dining table. My appreciation and love is extended with his wish that this be my last book, with the full knowledge he will have to endure the writing of more.

Tim Wilson, Melbourne, 11 May 2020

Introduction:

The vacuum and how to fill it

Popcorn politics

Popcorn politics is politics removed from philosophy; politics treated as consumer culture. Politics becomes filled with morsels of puffed-up ideas that are easy to digest and which provide instant gratification, but with so little intellectual nutrition that ultimately they don't make a meal. People can even get over excited and accidentally spill their surplus political opinions on the floor in the process. And when they're done, they've still got an appetite.

That's the descent of politics in Western liberal democracies over the last decade. It's been hastened by consumer behaviour that has reshaped people's political engagement. People look for easy, or at least easier, answers where there is only complexity. And too often, rather than appealing to principles and using persuasion, they throw out popcorn answers. It doesn't mean every answer that popcorn politics provides is wrong. It just means that such an answer doesn't equate to a meal. And nations don't survive on empty stomachs.

The enduring strength of the liberal project is that it provides a meal. It is a political philosophy for everyone: open, inclusive, and adaptable; a philosophy that can speak to—and improve—people's lived experience. But to be relevant for today, it has to adapt and address today's challenges. Yet it is missing in action.

The resurgence of socialist ideals amongst the young, and attempts to solve theoretical problems with technocratic solutions, is the latest wave of nationalist populism. This resurgence has meant the liberal project has lost its political cache. The threat of populism isn't just a local problem. It dogs every Western liberal democracy. Australia is not immune.

The perceived demise of liberalism is even reflected in our language. Traditionally, Australians on the centre-right always described themselves as some form of 'liberal'. It was largely anathema to describe yourself as a 'conservative'. When Sir Robert Menzies used the word 'conservative', it was normally as the butt of a joke at his own expense about his fondness for conservative landscape painting or Georgian architecture. In the context of politics, he often used it to mean something like what we associate with words like 'reactionary'. There will always be a live debate about the meaning of words, but it was clear that his understanding of liberalism was a focus on the future, and conservatism, a focus on the past.

The liberal brand

It's hard to think of a better brand than liberal. It stands for everything humanity aspires to: freedom, openness, tolerance, and empowerment.

Today, people aspire, however, to the moniker of conservatism as a reflection of their purity. 'Conservative' has displaced 'liberal' when discussing the alternative to 'social democracy' in Australia. So much so that, when Senator Cory Bernardi sought to establish a new political party after leaving the Liberal Party, he established the Australian Conservatives as a brand that his supporters would recognise as a purer vision of the centre-right movement. Yet he led it all the way through from its incubation to failure and deregistration. Ideological conservatism simply has little to offer Australians.

Though it is anchored in a cultural and legal context, liberalism is not a conservative outlook on the world. When the instinctive response to questions of public policy reform, from someone who identified as liberal, is against any change, it suggests an existential crisis surrounds the capacity of liberals to understand how to apply their philosophy in order to meet contemporary challenges.

Australian liberalism has its own tradition. An open political philosophy will always have followers who apply different emphases, and weigh up answers differently. But at its core is an interest in the future progress of our country and its people. Australian liberalism has traditionally spoken to the aspirations of the country primarily because it has focused on improving the lives of individuals. The ideas of liberalism still do. But there is clearly a difference between the ideas of liberalism and how it is sometimes practiced, and whether policy that is invoked in its name has a genuine connection with it. If liberalism can't find a constituency and solve contemporary challenges, then it will eventually be displaced from its podium.

This is not a recent phenomenon. The crisis confronting liberalism stems from a fundamental failure to rethink its purpose in the modern world. Liberalism won the battles of the twentieth century. It created much of the opportunity and progress that underpins the twenty-first century. But, rather than compounding its wins over the failure of other political philosophies, it seems to have fallen for its own success, become complacent, and not invested in reassessment and proposing liberal solutions to contemporary challenges.

Reassessing liberalism's purpose

The last time liberals properly assessed their ideological purpose and stoked the torch of liberty was in the 1970s. Despite the fact that liberal ideas were applied for thirty years, from the late 1980s through to the global financial crisis, providing an era of growth, the liberal torch no longer burns so brightly. It often seems only to flicker. Liberalism is no longer the default position. Liberalism is not losing the contest of ideas *per se*. The challenge is that the philosophy of liberalism is not being applied, and that failure is causing the constituency of people most likely to adopt a liberal outlook to decline it. Political philosophies may not need constituencies to survive, but its practical application does. A constituency that shares the values that underpin it, and a constituency that sees their interests advance through its practical application. And for liberalism—both are in retreat.

Forty years on, the generations coming through don't remember the Berlin Wall, protectionism, or recessions. In 2020, the last recession was nearly three decades ago. Australians under the age of thirty have lived their whole lives not knowing the consequence of parents losing a job, struggling to pay the mortgage, relocating when they can't, and the pressure these place on families. And given that the first decade of most people's life is rarely filled with the consciousness of the complexities of the world that surrounds them, this lack of awareness is really true of all Australians under forty. That means they've grown up in an age of extreme prosperity; albeit one that has allowed economic growth to be taken for granted, enabling institutions that evolved over hundreds of years to be treated like dusty books on a shelf, and technological change to discard political products by simply swiping left or right for disapproval or approval like a dating app. And that vacuum has been filled with introspective social and cultural causes that do little to unite or advance society, and by environmentalism that discounts the necessity of economic growth.

One of the most disturbing trends in this generation is their complacency about democracy. Who can blame a generation who have only read about the ravages of communism or socialism in a history book? They've lived in an era in which democracy is viewed through its weakness and not its hard-fought strengths. Meanwhile, their alternative benchmark is Chinese authoritarianism that is fêted for its capacity to build fast rail in years and hospitals to respond to viruses within days; whereas the checks and balances in our system create roadblocks leading to a drift of democratic inertia.

The response of liberals has not been to reinforce liberalism's foundations. They have done what the rest of society has done in the absence of an external threat—pursued the enemy within. Cultural debates that are red meat to the base have been pursued because they're instinctive, simplistic, and create a moral dichotomy of right and wrong, but they do little to broaden the constituency. Many cultural debates have become like MacGuffins. MacGuffins are plot devices used in films that are necessary for plot, but have an irrelevant purpose overall. That doesn't mean cultural debates serve no purpose.

We need to defend our way of life. But going on cultural crusades is not the basis of a sustainable, forward-looking political movement that seeks to fulfil the ambitions of individuals' lives.

This was best encapsulated on Australia Day 2015. That was the day it was announced that Australia would consider re-establishing knights and dames. I remember what instinctively went through my mind scrolling the story on my phone: "I don't know whose priority this, but they have nothing to do with me." Such a quote could be wrongly interpreted as a gratuitous criticism. But that is not the intent. It was a good example of political capital spent unwisely, and precisely because it was a needless fight that drew the wrong 'battlelines'.

That gut response had nothing to do with views on the structure of the Australian honours system. It was a message of priorities. And if that was how I was feeling, as a lifelong liberal and Liberal, the public reaction was predictable. It was clear who it was designed to speak to, and it wasn't to those who focused on the future of Australia.

Similarly, social debates are occasionally chosen because they can pump the blood of activists. Yet a core strength of liberalism is its universality. It is a political philosophy that, put into practice, empowers everyone to pursue their life, opportunity, and enterprise. When debates are pursued that isolate liberalism's universality, liberalism's appeal is corroded with it; and in a nation where a philosophy and political party share the same moniker, the negative correlation is shared.

By pursuing distractions, the Liberal Party has often wandered onto the political playing field without realising that the goal posts have been moving. Once upon a time, the goal posts were in the east and west of the field; and that's where they've been kicking for a goal.

Yet, every year, the goal posts have been moving a little further to the north and south. Now, even when many Liberal Party players kick the perfect shot, it rarely ends in the net because the goalposts have moved so far.

Speaking to a new generation

Our opponents have noticed. Recent election defeats might suggest otherwise, but they're playing the field that the emerging Australians are on. They're just ahead of the demographic shift. The largest demographic group by age today is no longer asset-owning Baby Boomers. Whether we call them 'millennials' or 'Generation Y', they are 18-35-year-olds looking for their opportunity.

The things young Australians are looking for are liberal—not that they'd know it. While younger Australians have worried about housing affordability, the Liberal Party has been talking up sustaining house prices. And while younger Australians are concerned about climate change, the Liberal Party talks of the necessity of mining industries as the foundation of the economy. Primary industries matter, but so does the financial security of homeownership. The economic consequences of Covid-19 will likely lead young Australians to be less concerned about climate change and more concerned about housing affordability and having a job. The Liberal Party's hope is that such a plight shouldn't face young Australians, and if it must, it does so temporarily. We should want the next generation of Australians to be able to stand on their own two feet, and then be focused on horizons beyond their simple survival.

When issues important to the next generation of Australians are addressed, they're addressed by those who lack the cultural relevance or cache to connect. Credibility matters. No one much cares about someone's solution to a problem when the proponent of the solution doesn't take the problem seriously. That leaves the full diversity of arguments put forward by economic socialists, cultural progressives, and environmental authoritarians to be let loose without credible scrutiny. Their views have been on the offensive, while Australian liberals are left defending their retreating territory and are simply being pounded by the weight of the waves of these compounding aggressive movements. It has got to stop. To advance liberalism you have to set the agenda, not merely play defence.

As this book will outline, the challenge liberals face is the challenge of a constituency in decline. The Liberal Party's constituency is ageing, declining in number, and hasn't bridged connections to find salience with a new demographic. And while the constituency of the Liberal Party and liberalism are not always identical, the constituency for those who see the value in advancing liberalism will find it their natural political home. Like any political philosophy in a democracy, liberalism needs a constituency who see its value if it is to successfully implement its ideals through practical policy. To do so, every political philosophy goes through stages of reassessing how it can be practically implemented to address contemporary issues. The principles remain the same. The evolution and re-imagination is in policy and how to map the path between the present and policy outcomes. Yet the enduring principles of liberalism—freedom, justice, and responsibility—are the answers to the challenges faced by the next generation of Australians. Too often what is absent is the visibility of challenges facing the new generation of Australians and liberal answers.

Conservatism offers little to this emerging generation of Australians.

The oddity is that the aspiration of young Australians is not radically different from their forebears. They want their own opportunity to shine. They were born into a 'bigger world' than their forebears, as a result of modern technology and communications. Their awareness of other cultures, environmental and scientific challenges, and injustices transcends their own lived experience. It's not surprising that they are looking for opportunity and intergenerational equity. What they want is their own 'fair go'. And what they perceive is that it is denied. Their homeownership rate is low. They're saddled with debt. The tax system plunders their income. They're deferring marriage and having a family. And even their employment is now on the line. They have little stake in contemporary Australia, so what does conservatism offer to them but seemingly more of little or nothing? Liberalism does offer them something. And they're looking for opportunities that only liberal democracy and the free market can provide.

Addressing practical challenges

Liberals must respond and connect their values to address these practical challenges. Left unaddressed, the risk is that young Australians will lose faith that our society, economy, and democracy works for them. Faith in democracy is already on a downhill trajectory and, in response, a hybrid of socialist populism has emerged. In the United Kingdom, these movements have found a voice in Baby Boomer socialists who emerged during the Cold War. The champion in the United Kingdom was Jeremy Corbyn, and, in the United States, it was Bernie Sanders. Both failed in electoral terms, but the issues that turned into a wave of popular support amongst young voters have not gone away. These issues will find new champions, as the rising popularity of Alexandria Ocasio-Cortez has shown. These trends have found multiple homes in Australia in the Greens and in parts of the Labor Party. They presently lack two things: first, a credible champion; and, second, economic circumstances that have brought them to the political fore overseas. Nearly thirty years of uninterrupted growth has enabled many economic problems to be papered over, and tempered aspirational young Australians' capacity to advance their private interests through working within the existing order. It is when the economic music stops, as it has now, that this could end. The response isn't likely to be a run on pitchforks at Bunnings. The risk is a soft revolution through the ballot box that knocks Australia off the liberal democratic path for the empty promise of the social democratic alternative.

This book starts the conversation about the pathway to repair. It is not a work about the big picture or one that paints 'that vision thing'. It's foundational. If we don't get the foundations right, the house can never be built. Australia has a liberal house. Most of our modern history has been building its foundations. But we have let them corrode. This book is an argument to fix them while we still can. What is needed is a liberal restoration by acknowledging liberalism's past, how it influenced and shaped the development of our country, and, frankly, how getting back to basics will make liberalism relevant again.

The book can be broken down into four sections. The first quarter (Chapters 1 and 2) focuses on defining liberalism and what it means. Liberalism has many branches, and it is important to understand how the modern Australian tradition developed against the backdrop of our history, provide some clarity about the modern liberalism that Menzies espoused and what relevance it has today. The second quarter (Chapters 3 and 4) focuses on what happened to liberalism over the past thirty years (a period I non-pejoratively call the era of equity extraction). Critically, it explores how liberalism became focused on the 'freedom of the individual', and how and why it needs to get back to focusing on the 'empowerment of the individual' to have a social licence. Importantly, that liberalism needs to reconnect with liberal concepts of justice to help guide solutions to challenges presented today. The third quarter (Chapters 5, 6 and 7) looks at why liberalism needs to refocus back onto the empowerment of the individual out of demographic necessity if it wants to have electoral appeal, particularly because of the direct connection between identifying with the values of liberalism and homeownership. And the fourth quarter (Chapter 8 and the Conclusion) is interested in how empowerment of the individual and home ownership provides for advancing of one of the most important protections for individuals and their freedom—decentralisation—to write a new Australian social contract with liberalism at its heart.

The Liberal Party and liberalism

Australian liberalism has many strands, and weaves into different parts of our political traditions and parties. The modern Liberal Party is the primary home of the Australian liberal tradition, but it doesn't have a monopoly. As you will read, traditions of liberalism can be found in other parties too. I've done my best to distinguish between the 'Liberal Party of Australia' or 'Liberals' and 'liberals' and 'liberalism', but it can get a little confusing; so when I write of the 'Liberal Party' it should be interpreted as partisan, and 'Australian liberals' or 'liberalism' should be interpreted as the political philosophy underpinning the Liberal Party. And it's important to acknowledge that not everyone in the Liberal Party necessarily identifies as ideologically liberal. Australian liberalism is bigger than any one person, or party. Its evolution is the story of our country.

Since its modern foundation, Australia has been a grand liberal experiment; an experiment that takes ideas and applies them practically. The ongoing success of the liberal project lies not only in handing it on from one generation to the next, but in making the project seem relevant to subsequent generations. That requires every generation to have a stake in liberalism's preservation for, as the former American President Ronald Reagan once said, "freedom is never more than one generation away from extinction".

What Australians are seeking is a new social contract—and only a restoration of liberal thought put into practice can deliver it.

1

The evolution of empowerment

A unique ideology

Liberalism is the most unique of all political ideologies. Almost every other political ideology has waxed and waned in response to events or been found wanting in its capacity to deliver for people. And that is what makes liberalism different: it is for people, or more precisely for individuals. Every other political ideology is focused in some way on the concentration of political, economic, social, or cultural power (intentionally or otherwise in the hands of the few) to achieve a grand purpose—whether it is confronting social disadvantage, environmental protection, national or religious conformity or order. Liberalism is the complete reverse. Liberalism is focused on keeping systems open to decentralise decision-making to individuals and the voluntary organic institutions they develop to drive their advancement: family, community, and enterprise. And, in doing so, individuals are empowered to take responsibility for their lives through the freedom to make choices.

There will always be movements, causes, and individuals who want to empower themselves. Since the end of the Cold War, the liberal democratic order was assumed to be the default (consistent with political scientist Francis Fukuyama's pronouncement of "the end of history"). There has been an under-investment in contributions on liberalism and how it must confront contemporary challenges. For liberalism to survive as a political ideology, it must live in the hearts and minds of the individuals it benefits.

In recent years, the brand of liberalism that has come to represent such a breadth of differing political views can be confusing, and it can vary markedly, depending on the time and context in which it is discussed. The consequence has been that liberalism has become a political ideology that can as easily be maligned by its enemies as it is celebrated by its friends. It has led to differing traditions that have recalibrated priorities away from the core objective of liberalism, and its commitment to empowering individuals, toward a narrow understanding of individualism, an overemphasis on freedom for the individual, and disengagement with issues surrounding equity and justice in society. Instead of being seen as a broad ideology that necessitates an active engagement in public policy decision-making that recalibrates laws, regulations, and programs to advance individual empowerment, it is interpreted as narrow and primarily resistant to the expansion of government even when reform may advance liberal objectives. This is not sustainable for any political ideology in a contest of ideas, and risks not having mature and saleable answers to the challenges that confront contemporary Australia.

Defining liberalism

Liberalism has a self-fulfilling genealogy. It means openness, and sourcing its origins is equally open. In *Liberalism: The life of an idea*, a former columnist for *The Economist*, Edmund Fawcett, argued that "liberalism has no foundation myth or year of birth, [instead] its intellectual and moral sources go back as far as energy or curiosity will take you".[1] Liberalism lacks an equivalent of Karl Marx's *Communist Manifesto*. It is the compounding influences of the evolutionary lessons of sovereign and executive overreach, populist uprisings, and settlements between the governing group and the governed. Liberalism's textbooks are the amalgam of works such as John Locke's *A Letter on Toleration* and John Stuart Mill's *On Liberty* on rights and respect for individuality, Adam Smith's *The Wealth of Nations* on private enterprise and his *The Theory of Moral Sentiments* on social order, and Charles-Louis Montesquieu's *The Spirit of Laws* on dividing power, among many others. Without a single political bible, everyone is free to interpret and weight the competing ideas that sit at its heart.

In *The Making of Modern Liberalism*, political theorist Alan Ryan observes, "Anyone trying to give a brief account of liberalism is immediately faced with an embarrassing question: are we dealing with liberalism or with liberalisms?"[2] As the different traditions—from the classical to what he describes as the modern—"do not agree about the boundaries of toleration, the legitimacy of the welfare state, and the virtues of democracy . . . they do not even agree on the nature of the liberty they think liberals ought to seek".[3]

In contemporary discussion, liberalism can be associated with 'classical liberalism', 'neo-liberalism', 'international liberalism', or 'modern liberalism', each of which reflect contextual debates about times, places, and issues. It can also include libertarianism.

Classical liberalism refers to a laissez-faire nineteenth-century understanding of liberalism anchored in private property, free trade, and freedom of conscience, expression, and religion. Ryan describes classical liberalism as embracing the liberalism espoused by Locke, Smith, de Tocqueville, and Hayek; a liberalism that "focuses on the idea of limited government, the maintenance of the rule of law, the avoidance of arbitrary and discretionary power, the sanctity of private property and freely made contracts, and the responsibility of individuals for their own fates".[4]

Essentially all forms of liberalism have a direct genealogical connection back to classical liberalism. And in the nineteenth and twentieth centuries they departed based on the contexts and events of individual countries.

Then there is 'international liberalism'. International liberalism is a distinct field of international relations theory that focuses on international cooperation through an appeal to common humanity, particularly through international institutions.

There may be no single definition of liberalism, but the constituent theme of the various branches of liberalism is its focus on the empowerment of individuals. Today:

- **Classical liberalism** is a belief in limited government because classical liberals recognise the threat of an overpowering arbitrary state against individual liberty, but also understand the importance of equality of opportunity for empowered individuals to exercise their social, political, and economic freedom, and their freedom to choose and take responsibility.

- **Libertarianism** is essentially a derivative of classical liberalism that narrowly prioritises the empowerment of the freedom of the individual and small government to protect property. Due to the cooption of a brand of liberalism in the United States in the nineteenth century by the progressive movements, libertarianism is used to distinguish a narrow understanding of classical liberalism from modern American progressive liberalism as well as moral conservatism.

- **Neo-liberalism** correlates with the late twentieth-century movements to promote competition by unwinding Keynesian restrictions on the market allocation of resources, privatisation of public corporations, removing protectionism and the promotion of free trade. It is also aligned with technological innovation and global economic integration that empowered capital and talent mobility.

- **Modern progressive liberalism** has differences in each country reflecting their own unique circumstances, but is a branch of liberalism focused on addressing inequities that disempowers individuals and collectives because of economic and social disadvantage. Modern progressive liberalism has its genealogy in early 20th Century progressive movements that diverted liberalism in countries like the United States, Canada and Britain, but less so in Australia.

- **Modern Australian liberalism** is focused on how to foster the environment for individuals to live out their best lives—respect for the equality and dignity of the individual, their freedom to take responsibility in pursuit of their life and enterprise, and the necessity of justice to respect that pursuit.

The meaning of modern liberalism really depends on the country. In the United Kingdom the classical liberal tradition is more closely aligned with conservatism, with part of the classical liberal tradition separately branching off in the twentieth century and finding accommodation with democratic socialism. In a partisan sense this modern progressive liberal tradition is represented by the modern Liberal Democrats who focus on both equality of opportunity, addressing historical inequities as well as respecting collective identity.

Modern American liberalism reflects influences of the Scottish and French Enlightenment that informed the foundation of their republic, as well as their own political history: the legacy of slavery and the civil war, immigration, race-based politics and concentrations of economic power, the anti-trust movement, and the New Deal, as well as the nineteenth-century progressive movement that led to phenomena such as the constitutional prohibition of alcohol, a lesser commitment to a free economy, and focused more closely on personal fulfilment. Today modern American liberalism is closely associated with the Democratic Party.

Similarly, in Canada, modern liberalism is also associated closely with progressivism. Progressivism ranges from a diversity of forms of social solidarity through trade unionism and government-driven equity programs to the more recent adoption of radical identity politics. In practice, these values have found their home in Canada's Liberal Party.

Ryan argues that, in America, Britain and Canada (as distinct from

Australia), modern liberalism

> reverses the ambitions and restraints of classical liberalism . . . [and]
> is exemplified by John Stuart Mill's *On liberty*, with its appeal to 'man
> as a progressive being' and its romantic appeal to individuality that
> should be allowed to develop itself in all its 'manifold diversity' . . .
> [yet] does not share the antipathies and hopes of a socialist defence
> of the modern welfare state … [but] in practice, it is exemplified by
> the assault on freedom of contract and the on the sanctity of property
> rights represented by the welfare legislation of the Liberal government
> in the UK before World War I, by Franklin Roosevelt's New Deal
> between the wars, and by the explosion of welfare-state activity after
> World War II.[5]

Most of what Australians view as liberalism follows from the evolution of the English and Scottish traditions. Today, its meaning orbits around its classical meaning of a political philosophy that places the individual at the heart of the society and economy; a position that enables the individual to live free, government to be limited, and the economy and society to be open. Australian liberalism is a variant of modern liberalism more closely aligned to classical liberalism than American modern liberalism. Like classical liberalism, modern Australian liberalism focuses on the empowerment of the individual. Unlike classical liberalism, it has made peace with the necessity of a liberal social justice to advance equality of opportunity and round the sharp edges of a dynamic market economy.

The non-ideological culture of Australia recognises the theoretical and practical shortcomings of libertarianism. For many Australians libertarianism is reflected by American venture capitalist, Joe Lonsdale, who argues it "has become a useless, purely performative sort of politics [with] many libertarians . . . blinded to the fact that the American social contract has fundamentally changed in character . . .

but while libertarianism has become a form of unhelpful critique, liberty remains as vital as ever before".[6]

Australian liberalism recognises that libertarianism appeals to individualist purity in a complex contemporary world; a world that has to confront concentrations of power against individuals, such as from government, corporations, and cultural forces. Therefore, modern liberalism in Australia understands that it is not freedom that matters as an end in itself, but the empowerment of the individual and their freedom to choose and take responsibility.

Liberalism's radical idea

Any proper appreciation of either classical or modern liberalism requires an understanding of just how radical the idea of the individual is. For most of human history, concern for the small (think 'family') and large (think 'body politic') collective was the norm. It was not just how communities survived against threats from each other and nature, but also culturally ingrained from the organic relationships—family units—and their interaction with one another as the foundation of society. In *Inventing the Individual*, Larry Siedentop explains that, in pre-Christian Western societies, family was the means of identification and ancient concepts of liberty were closely associated with inclusion in the collective:

> Ancient liberty consisted of having a share in the government of the city, in public power. It consisted of the privilege and duty to attend the assembly, speak in debates, judge the arguments, takes sides and vote, with the further possibility of serving as a magistrate or on a jury, if required. Ancient liberty did not tolerate indifference to the political process. The public thing, res publica, was everything.[7]

The radical proposition of individuality depended upon changes in people's understanding of their familial bonds and, through these, their relationship with a broader community. While there was no single cause of this, the development of Christian thought was key to it. Christianity turned relationships and morality between families and communities with family or community gods, into relationships between individuals and a monotheistic God. Christians invoked "'the country of god' to assert the claims of the individual conscience. Such claims of conscience seemed to follow irresistibly from the assumption of moral equality. Equality, choice and responsibility hung together in their minds".[8]

The very foundation from Christ through "baptism, after all, was of individuals. Only God could 'own souls'. This new universality—the attributing of conscience and will to 'all souls'—helped to sound the death knell of ancient slavery".[9] And Christianity's "concern for the individual soul and its fate loomed ever larger, [as demonstrated through] the high price paid for Christian emphasis on human equality and the claims of conscience".[10] As Christianity and Western society evolved, these ideas were reflected in the gradual shift in attitudes toward authority:

> it stipulated that all 'persons' should be considered as 'individuals', in that they share an underlying equality of status as children of god. Instead of traditional social inequalities being deemed natural—and therefore not needing justification—an underlying moral equality was now deemed natural. This reversal of assumptions meant that paterfamilias and lordship were no longer 'brute' facts that stood outside and constrained the claims of justice. They too were now subject to the scrutiny of justice.[11]

And shifting concepts of justice and law led Christians to shape society:

Appealing to 'nature' or natural law (*jus naturale*) as the foundation of justice rapidly became standard for the canonists. For example, they defended the new forms of legal procedure designed to permit a fair trial in those terms . . . the canonists' egalitarian concern for individual conscience and free will led them gradually to recast natural law as a system of natural rights: pre-social or moral rights inhering in the individual. In that way, the canonists converted the primordial Christian concern with 'innerness' into the language of law. That conversion laid the foundation of modern liberalism.[12]

This conversion led to a broader consideration of the importance of natural rights that extended to conscience and property, as well as process rights in systems of justice and the foundations of much of the modern conception of a liberal order. So the advent of Christianity is not sufficient to explain the modern liberal democratic order without an understanding of this broader discussion that it stimulated.

These ideals informed the cultural makeup of societies, particularly in the British Isles. The conception of individuality and the dignity of the individual was located at the cultural heart of major socio-political developments which depended upon understandings of the individual's relationship to the collective and the state. The eight-hundred-year-old Magna Carta continues to have a mystique because of its association with the genesis of a conception of a rights-based culture of liberty and protection of the individual against the state. As a former Conservative Member of the European Parliament, Daniel Hannan, writes of Magna Carta in *How we invented freedom and why it matters*:

> the English speaking peoples have tended to treat that text as their Torah, the script that sets them apart . . . Lord Denning, the most celebrated of all Twentieth-Century English jurists, declared: "Magna

Carta is the greatest constitutional document of all times—the foundation of the freedom of the individual against the arbitrary authority of the despot.[13]

Magna Carta included many principles that went on to inform the development of contemporary society—consensual taxation, equality before the law, and fair justice. And, although it applied only to a small number of noblemen, Hannan explains that its legacy for liberalism is its understanding of the relationship between the individual in relation to the state. Whether through the empowerment of a monarch or a parliament, the power of the state is to impose its will onto people with the ultimate backstop of violence and force for non-compliance, and against the freedom of the individual to take responsibility. On a spectrum, if the state is empowered and takes responsibility, then the individual is almost always disempowered, must conform, and loses their freedom to take responsibility. Or put more simply—big government makes for small citizens.

The enemy of monopoly

The underlying theme of liberalism is actually a discussion about power; and ultimately that centralised and monopolistic systems of government power, social structures and order, and economic institutions should be designed to decentralise power and prefer the distribution of power toward individuals and their freedom to choose and take responsibility. This empowerment of individuals comes through decentralisation of all forms of power, and affirming respect for:

- individuality and the assumption that people are free to exercise their fundamental freedoms of conscience, religion, speech, association, and ownership of property, and that constraints upon these should be narrowly sanctioned by consensual law (an assumption not shared by states that legally regulate behaviour, use censorship, and rely upon compulsion);

- individual economic empowerment and advancement through private ownership, the individual's freedom to trade in a competitive market informed by price signals that inform supply and demand, as well as free and open exchange in a marketplace of ideas to promote progress and scientific advancement (empowerment not enjoyed within states that embrace collective ownership and centralised planning);

- individual political power through the universal franchise and the freedom to stand for election and form alternative political parties in a competitive democracy that forms consensual laws (power that is denied in states subject to dictatorship or constraints on electoral participation);

- individual protection from coercion of monopolistic and authoritarian government through competitive governance, including the division of formal powers between parliaments, the executive and courts, as well as between localised authorities and central governments, to ensure choice in governance and decisions made closest to the people they serve, and informal power balanced between government, a free press, and civil society to hold democratic governments accountable (protections that are diminished by state-approved and funded organisations).

These ideas are not solely the monopoly of liberalism. Socialism has a tradition of 'rights', but mostly through the idea of rights afforded by the state. Religious faiths, such as Catholicism, have a tradition of local empowerment through subsidiarity. But no other political ideology brings these ideas together coherently with the objective of empowerment of the individual.

In *The Economist's* essay, "Some thoughts on the crisis of liberalism— and how to fix it", authored under the nom-de-plume Bagehot, liberalism is explained in terms of a "delicate balance between four opposing sets of principles: (1) elitism and democracy, (2) top-down management and self-organisation, (3) globalism and localism, and (4) what might be termed, for simplicity's sake, the hard and the soft"— opaquely meaning the rigidity of rules, institutions, and scientific laws as opposed to culture, community, and spontaneous order.[14]

Bagehot is only partly right. It isn't so much as a delicate balance between these opposing principles, as much as an acknowledgement of the necessity of the former and the ambition for the latter. At its heart, liberalism has a constant dissonance that history has taught us needs to be tempered.

Liberals recognise that power imbalances are a reality, but the ambition is for informed and considered government that enjoys social licence through democratic legitimacy. Liberalism can accommodate the reality that top-down power is necessary to create the framework for the operation of a society and economy, but dynamism, innovation, and progress come from spontaneous order, voluntary exchange and participation, and competition. Although global cooperation for economic prosperity, peace, and environmental stewardship requires a community of nations to work together, the solution to this collaboration originates with responsible and consenting citizens and communities to justify national policy. And while rigidity in rules is sometimes necessary to provide clear boundaries, unnecessarily rigid rules can also be stifling. So we need to free people to conduct themselves with respect for others, and for laws of all kinds. In this way, we need never limit the creativity and breadth of what humanity aspires to achieve.

Liberalism is the practical application of political ideology that observes the human condition, channels human instincts, and curtails human shortcomings. It builds a culture and institutions that respect each person's fundamental equality and dignity and empowers individuals, but which also leaves them free to take the responsibility to pursue their life, opportunity, and enterprise.

Liberalism's universality also ensures it has a broad global constituency. Almost every country has some liberal movement applied to their unique context, and sometimes as a radical alternative to traditions of cultural collectivism.

2

Australian liberalism

Beginnings of Australian liberalism

The origin of the Australian liberal experiment was an application of the contemporary ideas and debates germinating in Europe. Ideas were debated and implemented through colonial institutions and law, and subsequently those of the Commonwealth after Federation. Liberalism underpins the Australian way of life because it is not a reaction to a pre-existing order: it was able to develop organically as the nation developed with its own culture. As such, it reflects our unique conditions as a nation.

No Australian had sought to narrate the full breadth of that story until the former cabinet minister and political historian, David Kemp, put pen to paper. Kemp has become the custodian of the liberal tradition for Australia. His series on the Australian liberal tradition contains: *The Land of Dreams 1788-1860*, *A Free Country 1860-1901*, and *A Democratic Nation 1901-1925*, with future volumes in prospect. In *The Land of Dreams*, Kemp writes:

> Australia has indeed been a liberal project since its [modern] foundation. Australians can scarcely begin to understand the country in which they live without a grasp of the nature of this project, and of those who originated it, developed it, and sought to apply its ideas to the government of a nation.[1]

Australian liberalism is unique. Its incubation began after the authorship of writings and the occurrence of events that shaped the liberal traditions, whose ideas were applied in the British Isles, European societies and the United States. Instead, Australia had the luxury of learning from the practical application of liberal intellectual thought. It was influenced by European theorists, and a consideration of how their thinking could be applied in a very different context. Australian liberals weren't presented with a pre-existing modern political order. They were presented with the relatively blank canvas of a new continent. (Admittedly, it was blank because they did not engage with the pre-existing culture of its indigenous peoples.) Australian liberalism also didn't develop as a response to the legacy of feudalism and a class-based system, or in response to revolution fought in pursuit of protecting the individual from tyranny. In other countries, to be liberal was a statement against an existing order, whereas, as the political scientist, Timothy Lynch, succinctly explains, "Australia is one of the few countries in the world where one can call oneself a liberal and mean it".[2]

Australian liberalism developed organically as an experiment in the application of contemporary ideas circulating widely in Europe around the time Europeans arrived in Australia, and the new colonies became the petri dish for their unshackled application. In their essay on *Liberalism and the Australian Federation*, former Liberal minister and party president, Tony Staley, and political scholar, John Nethercote, state:

In Australia, Liberalism has virtually never been defined in ideological or even doctrinal terms. It has always . . . embraced a range of values central to the political, social and economic life of the nation. Prominent among these values are constitutionalism, representative and responsible government, bicameralism and federalism—this latter value is perhaps the most distinctive value in Australian liberalism for it expresses, in a practical way, an opposition to concentration of power and a desire for its dispersal to other democratically based governments. Whether in the political, social or economic spheres of life, Australian Liberalism has supported and advocated the rights and freedoms of individuals, especially when threatened by collectivist views and organization . . . Toleration is a key instrumental value in fostering an environment in which these liberties can be realised.[3]

The founder of the modern Liberal Party of Australia, Sir Robert Menzies, took a similar approach, arguing that Australian liberalism lacked a 'doctrinaire' approach, when compared to the ideological rigidity of socialism. In a 1964 speech to the Federal Council of the Liberal Party, he said:

We have no doctrinaire political philosophy. Where government action or control has seemed to us to be the best answer to a practical problem, we have adopted that answer at the risk of being called Socialists. But our first impulse is always to seek the private enterprise answer to help the individual to help himself, to create a climate, economic, social, industrial, favourable to his activity and grow it. Our opponents have an exactly opposite point of approach. Their first instinct is the Socialist one. "The right way to deal with this matter is for the Government to run it!" Private enterprise and effort are the alternatives to which they reluctantly turn only when the Socialist plan proves to be constitutionally incompetent or in practice unworkable.[4]

In his Tocquevillian essay, "Political ideology in Australia: The distinctiveness of a Benthamite society", the British lawyer, Hugh

Collins, observes that European liberalism could not be simply "transplanted" and that the continent confronted settlers with a "new environment [that] altered them and their politics, even as they reproduced the parliamentary procedures and party labels of British politics. The best-educated and most self-conscious of the colonial liberals, C. H. Pearson, acknowledged this when he referred to his first experience of settlement in Australia as having changed him from a 'liberal of the English type to a democratic liberal'."[5]

Federation as a liberal project

While the debates surrounding Federation often broke down into interests of the soon-to-be-States, liberals were divided between those for free trade, led from New South Wales, and Melbourne protectionists. As Kemp chronicles, the Australian colonial era was a century-long discussion about the evolution and application of liberal ideas in and for the Australian continent. In his essay on *Liberalism: The International Context*, the political historian, Chandran Kukathas, acknowledges that "Australian liberalism was not born with federation but was already in operation in the constitutions of the various colonies in the nineteenth century", but that "the Constitution is the most substantial statement of Australian liberalism".[6]

The Federation project does not create a tight legal framework for the operation of a democracy. Rather, it is primarily an expression of respect for individuals and their freedom, and the institutions necessary to secure such freedom. It leaves questions about the limits of the state and people's relationship to one another for ongoing democratic debate. The Australian Constitution lacks rigidity, except for the high threshold of its amendment mechanism, requiring a double majority of both the consent of the people and the States. Unlike the American Bill of Rights, which imposes strong limitations on government and the laws that the Congress can make, the Australian Constitution primarily divides power between the States and the Commonwealth, and puts few limits on the expanse of legislative or executive power. The rights-based individualism more closely associated with libertarianism, which is narrow in its focus, and doctrinal in its approach toward freedom at the expense of the individual is not present. In Australia, our democracy was to be a constant conversation to advance individual empowerment within wide boundaries, not limited by rigid rights-based individualism.

At this point, Australian liberalism carries common heritage with traditions reminiscent of those within the United Kingdom. It was the federation of the Australian colonies into the Commonwealth that institutionalised uniform liberal principles across the continent.

The ideas of liberalism are infused in the Constitution itself, including religious tolerance, protection for private property, free trade between the States, the separation of powers, and competitive federalism. Each is central to the continuation of a liberal nation under a constitution. Religious tolerance through the limits of the federal government to sanction religion and impose a religious test respects fundamental freedoms of conscience, expression, and association, as well as the development of non-state sources of authority to protect individuals against the arbitrary power of the state. Free trade between the States is a direct expression of a domestic free market economy with private ownership and enterprise at its core. The separation of powers reflects the need to hold government accountable to a democratically elected legislature and the courts' interpretations through the common law that assumes individual liberty. And competitive federalism both devolves power away from national capitals to State capitals, and reduces the power distance between government and individuals to bring about change in a democracy. Doing so also creates a competitive environment of laws and administration, enabling citizens not just the choice to exercise their voice about the laws that they wish to be bound by, but also the freedom to move to another political community if its laws better reflect their values, and to constrain Commonwealth power to matters of standardisation and Australia's relationship with the rest of the world.

The design of the Australian federation began with reflections on the American experience of federalism, but it also uniquely formed from a distinctive geography and history of six colonies that voluntarily chose this destiny without the need for a revolution or the decision of an imperial power. Australia's unique geography made unitary government completely unresponsive to localised challenges (particularly given the technology of the time), as well as base understanding that government is reflective of, and responsive to the people it serves when it is closest to them. Representatives, even from a community, in a national capital will always have to bargain about priorities and issues with others who have different concerns and therefore decisions will be broad in their focus, distant in their proximity, bland in their uniformity, and slow in their making. By comparison, localised decision-making will always be more reflective of community sentiment and values, responsive to shifting community sentiment, and more precise in its capacity to address local circumstances.

Economic decentralisation is equally important from a liberal perspective. There are many good economic arguments around the efficient use of capital and resources to justify private property and free enterprise, but its enduring strength is the economic decentralisation of economic power from the hands of the few to the empowerment of every individual. Private property confers the capacity for individuals to exploit and trade their labour and goods. The challenge for liberals, as with all concentrations of power, is around the parameters of when the advantages of concentration of power, including from efficiency, capacity to leverage for future investments, and collaboration, outweigh the benefits and risk becoming predatory and undermining competition. The greater the democractisation of the economic wealth of the nation, the greater the sense of ownership ordinary citizens ultimately feel for the status quo as their vested stake in its interest and defining its future. As Kemp writes:

> A number of political movements in the nineteenth century were inspired by the dream of a classless society—not only the Australian liberals but also socialist, communist and even anarchist movements. These movements differ partly in what they meant by classlessness, but their differences primarily lay in their assessment of how to dismantle the old order . . . Liberals saw the road to a classless society through the promotion of an egalitarian democratic culture, broadening the ownership of private property, universal education and politics that secured the equal freedom of all to pursue their own goals in life".[7]

Individualism in Australia

The absence of a commitment to rigid individualism, which is more closely associated with a modern understanding of libertarianism, has allowed for a form of liberalism that extends beyond an exclusive commitment to freedom, and incorporates a form of justice that affords equal opportunity because of how it can advance the interests of individuals.

Collins, argued that Australia is a "curious mix of the familiar and foreign . . . if one begins by regarding Australia as a Benthamite society".[8] Collins's conclusion is built on the understanding that Jeremy Bentham's utilitarian instincts found a home in Australia and informed its evolution. Collins understands Betham's utilitarianism as follows:

> utilitarianism . . . [reconciles] the pursuit of individual interests with the achievement of the sovereign interest of greatest happiness . . . political institutions and policies are to be assessed in terms of their impact of their operation upon the interests of the majority—and that Bentham conceived not as groups or classes but as the sum of individual interests . . . [and] although the agenda of Bentham's utilitarian state includes issues that are now associated with a collectivist age, such as education and health, and welfare, in Bentham's system these tasks are firmly secure to individualist interests.[9]

Despite a concern for justice, Benthamite utilitarianism doesn't follow the direction of contemporary progressive liberalism and doesn't shift its focus from the protection of individual rights toward social or group rights. Thus, it remains relatively hostile to discussion of rights beyond those that belonging to all citizens as individuals. As Collins observes, "Although a theory of individual interests, it rejects the notion of natural rights which was central in both the American and the French revolutions . . . in an ideology faithful to Bentham's system, natural rights will be an alien tradition".[10]

Collins argues that Australians are equally hostile to social contract theory because it is anchored in conceptions of individual rights, which have limited appeal in the Australian tradition. That is partly true. The absence of a bill of rights explicitly rejected in the Constitution reflected the political culture that evolved to that point, and as witnessed in the Federation debates. However, the basic concept of civil and political rights flowed from the common law inherited from England and the transfer of Enlightenment ideas that came with European settlers. The rights-based culture of the American colonies flowed from the over-reach of British imperialism leading to their War of Independence. Westminster and monarchs learned from this experience. Therefore, the Australian colonies had a high degree of local autonomy, negating the need for reaction to an over-bearing distant imperial authority. The consequence has been that, although Australian liberalism values liberty, it is not seen as an end in itself in constant need of assertion. Rather, the objective of liberalism is individual empowerment.

Collins may argue Australians reject the notion of a narrow social contract anchored in the concept of natural rights, but that does not mean that Australians are hostile to a broader understanding of a social contract as the relationship between the citizen and the state. The Australian understanding of a social contract places limits and expectations on the state about how it seeks to empower individuals to live their fullest lives through a basic respect for equality of opportunity, deferral to individual responsibility, and utility— outcomes that enlarge these opportunities for the most number of people. As a result, there is a pragmatic understanding that liberty is a matter of advancing individual empowerment for the maximum number of people. Colloquially, we refer to it as a 'fair go', because it assumes both equality of opportunity and an expectation of individual freedom and responsibility, as well as constraint on those who would exploit their power to deny others their equal chance at happiness and success. Ordinarily, some of these aspirations would seem to be in conflict; that we must sacrifice one to achieve the other, but because Australian liberalism treats the individual as the nucleus around which political values revolve, it requires a constant re-evaluation to find their equilibrium with each other through democratic debate.

These ideas have consistently been tested throughout our modern history. The Eureka Rebellion reflected a stand by the self-employed against the abuse of power and over-taxation by the Crown. It was both an assertion of individual enterprise against an over-bearing state, and an assertion of government by consent. In 1902, respect for all citizens led to universal franchise, ensuring Australia was the first country to extend the opportunity for women to vote and stand for Parliament.[11] Freedom of association was challenged in Menzies's failed attempt to amend the Constitution to ban the Communist Party.

The introduction of the White Australia Policy was central to the post-Federation consensus that editor-at-large of *The Australian*, Paul Kelly, describes as the 'Australian settlement'. The Australian settlement was a social contract designed to advance the interests of individual citizens of the nation against perceived broader foreign threats. So too was that the dismantling of the policy, commenced under the Menzies and Holt government. This broadened the definition of who could be an Australian. It began to challenge the tyranny of racial and other forms of prejudice, as did the 1967 referendum to recognise Aboriginal and Torres Strait Islanders as full citizens, and the 2017 postal survey that led to the extension of marriage to include same-sex couples. In all cases, the liberal cause won: individuals triumphed over compulsion and suppression; individuals affirmed their dignity and mutual respect. The Australian journey has only gone in one direction: toward a fuller liberal conception of justice and empowerment for individuals.

What Menzies did

Australian history weaves a narrative of citizens negotiating the development of a liberal democracy designed to advance the interests of individual citizens, their families, and community as the foundation for the strength of the country. Nineteenth-century colonial debates were dominated by the application of liberal principles adapted to local conditions by people who found themselves in Australia by birth, choice, or compulsion. The latter part of the century was committed to uniting the colonies toward a federation with liberal ideals at its heart; a federation to be built and tested in the first half of the twentieth century by wars, economic depression, and social and political movements offering alternatives whose allure proved attractive in Europe and elsewhere. These were periods of significant debate about the formation of a modern country, and its direction.

The post-War era provided the foundations for a modern liberal society in peace.

Without doubt, the seismic event in the institutionalisation of Australian liberalism in post-War Australia was Sir Robert Menzies's unification of civil society organizations and political movements committed to liberal ideals to form the Liberal Party of Australia.

It is difficult to understate the significance of what Menzies and others created. Prior to Federation, colonial politics was dominated by liberal parties. The post-Federation formation of liberal parties was a tumultuous period. Fusion of the protectionists and free traders led to the creation of the Commonwealth Liberal Party in the first decade, but fragmentation in the Labor Party over conscription led to Labor dissidents joining with the CLP to form the Nationalist Party less than a decade later. The Nationalists only lasted slightly longer before being absorbed into the newly formed United Australia Party following another split in the Labor Party over its response to the Great Depression. The UAP only lasted a similar period lacking any clear guiding philosophy and purpose beyond electoral success. By the mid-1940s, the custodians of the Australian liberal tradition were in disarray with a Labor Party planning post-War reconstruction, including the public ownership of some industries, and the nationalisation of the banks.[12]

It took Menzies's preparedness to recognise the shortcomings of the UAP to unite a divergent group of non-Labor, non-socialist, nationalist, and liberal organizations under a single banner with a coherent political philosophy. Troy Bramston, the author of *Robert Menzies: The art of politics*, explains that the conference that founded the Liberal Party brought together:

> 77 delegates and observers from 18 centre-right organizations. The attendees included representatives from organizations such as the Institute of Public Affairs, the Australian Constitutional League, and the Australian Women's National League. There were state and federal parliamentarians, and officials from political parties such as the Nationalist Party, the Liberal Democratic Party, and the Services and Citizens Party.[13]

Bramston continues:

> Menzies argued that the new party had to have a "political faith" that would define what it stood for and provide a rallying point for action. He spoke of a party with "a liberal and progressive faith" that was neither reactive nor negative. It was essential that the party was not seen to be resistant to "political and economic progress" and "branded as reactionaries". The party's task had to be one of proposition, not just opposition. The party could not be an organization that simply said "no" or occupied a self-satisfied position as a "critic" of Labor's

policies. "There is no room in Australia for a party of reaction . . . [and] I see the individual and his encouragement and recognition as the prime motive force for the building of a better world," he said. Menzies spoke about security, opportunity, and prosperity for all citizens. And he addressed education, employment, housing, and industrial relations.[14]

Menzies brought together fractious civil society and political movements united in their opposition to democratic socialism and its political representation through the Labor Party. Together, they formed a political movement motivated to be the liberal alternative. In his address to the conference that united these movements, Menzies called for "a true revival of liberal thought which will work for social justice and security, for national power and national progress, and for the full development of the individual citizen, though not through the dull and deadening process of socialism".[15]

In his election speech, he distilled the new party's electoral platform. Menzies articulated the foundations of his party: to advance the cause of human freedoms "to worship, to think, to speak, to choose, to be ambitious, to be independent, to be industrious, to acquire skill, to seek reward".[16] Put simply, the realisation of the Australian liberal vision is of empowered individuals in all aspects of their life.

Menzies's observations of liberalism revealed the truly Australian nature of the tradition, and specifically acknowledged that "individual enterprise must drive us forward. That does not mean we are to return to the old and selfish notions of laissez-faire. The functions of the State will be much more than merely keeping the ring within which the competitors will fight".[17] This observation by Menzies is one of his most important. It reflects the context of the time in the post-War period, when the laissez-faire period of the late nineteenth and early twentieth centuries was still treated with suspicion. His observations also highlight a clear demarcation between liberalism for *individuals,* and liberalism for *individualism.* Menzies understood that the objective of public policy was not to foster a society of disconnected individualism, but a society of individuals who shared their mutual responsibility to each other and society as part of the pathway for individual fulfillment.

He also recognised that, while enterprise is essential to the liberal tradition, the objective of liberalism was not unfettered freedom in the domains of personal autonomy or commerce, but the cultivation of an environment that allowed individuals to flourish. And to the extent that economic or other interests undermined individuals' flourishing, liberal policymakers would choose the individual over other vested interests.

In the post-War reconstruction era, there was a genuine contest of ideas about the direction of the country. Menzies understood that in order for Australians to realise their individual fulfilment, the government needed to be able to articulate a clear plan of how a liberal vision could turn the philosophical to the practical:

> I believe that a large majority of the public today is perfectly ready to give its adherence to a party which will display political principle and political courage . . . We have suffered far too much from people who have no political convictions beyond a more or less genteel adherence to our side of politics. That kind of adherence is worthless. We must have people who believe things, and who are prepared to go out and struggle to make their beliefs universal.[18]

There are many conclusions that we should draw from Menzies's insight.

Menzies rejects the idea that it is an acceptable political position simply to be anti-socialist or anti-Labor. Unity in opposition is not a persuasive basis upon which to form government. Nor does it give supporters and parliamentarians guidance about a coherent position to form policy that would stir the enthusiasm of individual voters. The universal appeal of a political movement can only be realised when people can see their own lives lived through the values and aspirations projected. He believed that the unifying principle of a political movement has to aspire to success and cannot be merely anchored in middle-class sensibilities of the rejection of egregious indulgences of the alternative. Menzies understood that the wealthy can take care of themselves, that the poor would always attract compassion, and that workers were represented by the Labor Party and its entrenched interests. Thus, he understood that what unified his party; what it must articulate and fight for, is individuals: it must empower most Australians to achieve their aspirations. Critically, unlike the Labor platform to advance the sectional interest of working people, and particularly the unions that provide the membership base of the party, every individual would benefit from Menzies's liberal vision—even if the core of his electoral base was the middle-class 'forgotten people'.

Menzies understood that Australia was a country that should foster individual achievement, not a country of class divides and pre-determined destinies. It had a modern English inheritance in institutions and culture that should be conserved, but it was the responsibility of Australians to be:

> not only the inheritors but in our own fashion the creators, the people who continue the tradition, who build on it, who improve on it, who are not just reactionary in their minds, who look forward, who are free in their minds and enterprising in their thoughts, but who always know the foundations on which they build.[19]

And to then lead and define economic and social progress by

"greatly [aiding] social justice . . . [by encouraging] free enterprise, [by recognising] the making of a people as one of the dynamic inducements to the taking of capital risks in the development of the nation. But we have insisted upon the performance of social and industrial progress is not to be based upon the poverty of despair of those who cannot compete".[20]

That understanding of liberalism was not just ideological, but also practical. It was ideological because it understood that the social fabric of a nation depends on the strengths of bonds held between its citizens, particularly in a post-War era. Similarly, it appealed to a solidarity surrounding nationhood and against social fragmentation. He recognised that "within the limits of social justice and national necessity, private citizens ought to be encouraged to get on with the job free of the threat that if they succeed too well some socialist theorists will want to take them over . . . because a self-ordered country with responsible government, [is] a country in which extremists and the promotors of division and hatred die for want of material to sustain them".[21]

It was practical because advancing political ideals into law depends on building a political constituency who share those values, or at least see their interests advanced through them. If the Australian community could not see their futures advanced through the political product that the Liberal Party espoused, it had no chance of then being implemented.

Some of the ideals of social solidarity, nationhood, and social justice may seem alien to contemporary threads of liberalism, particularly libertarianism and neo-liberalism. Both place a higher importance on people's freedom to act and a lower importance on government action to address concentrations of power and imbalances that limit individuals. Menzies understood that government had a role in softening the edges of economic actors to empower citizens. He demonstrated his commitment to advancing individual empowerment throughout his career, from the time of his 1939 resignation from the Lyons government, for their failure to proceed with the National Insurance Act, to his later reflections on his own government in his second last year as Prime Minister:

> Our opponents thought that they had a monopoly of interest in social services, but you just look back on it and think of the things that we produced—not our opponents—the things that we produced, the innovations in this field: The Aged Persons Homes Act, one of the great social measures of our times . . . the Medical Health Scheme, the Pharmaceutical Scheme, housing loans, housing insurance.[22]

Consistent with the long tradition of Australian liberalism, Menzies understood that while it was desirable for citizens to take responsibility themselves, and that the private sector should be best left to solve its own problems, the government had a role in empowering individuals to be their best selves and stand on their own two feet.

This was a topic addressed by Menzies artfully in one of his *Forgotten People* speeches. The first five speeches of the series[23] focused on American President Franklin Roosevelt's concept of the 'four freedoms': freedom of speech, freedom of worship, freedom from want and freedom from fear. Roosevelt outlined the four freedoms in his 1941 State of the Union address and became the bedrock of the aspirations of the Atlantic Charter between Roosevelt and Churchill for a post Second World War era. The 'four freedoms' were fundamentally intertwined with the ideals of the post-Depression New Deal. The ideas of freedom of speech and worship were not new and are emblematic of British social and political theorist, Isaiah

Berlin's later analysis of *Two concepts of liberty*. Berlin divided liberty into negative liberty and positive liberty:

> I shall call the 'negative' sense, is involved in the answer to the question 'What is the area within which the subject—a person or group of persons—is or should be left to do or be what he is able to do or be, without interference by other persons?' The second, which I shall call the positive sense, is involved in the answer to the question 'What, or who, is the source of control or interference that can determine someone to do, or be, this rather than that?'[24]

Berlin argued that negative liberty is "the ability to do what one wishes" free from government coercion, which is consistent with freedom of speech and worship. Positive liberty is what someone needs to be empowered as an individual, and a clearer reflection of freedom from want and fear. The challenge particularly of freedom from want is that it can necessarily justify the enlargement of government to empower individuals but only through the burdensome taxation and regulation to achieve a socialist equality of outcome. Menzies's saw the limitations of the idea of freedom from want in his third Forgotten People speech on the subject:

> The arriving at a true answer to any difficult problem requires a just balancing of various factors. If our motto is to be, "Each for himself and the devil take the hindmost", then want will be the portion of the least active or the least fortunate, and our civilisation will be disfigured by those extremes of wealth and poverty, of comfort and despondency, which have defaced our history in the past, and which a proper understanding of human dignity will roundly condemn. But if the motto is to be that each citizen is entitled, whatever his own effort . . . all incentive to effort will vanish.[25]

The balance Menzies identified was to understand that the empowerment of the individual depended on responsibility and that:

My right to be free imposes on me obligations of the most absolute kind to defend my freedom. And so if I am to have freedom from want I must pay the price of that freedom. I must work and strive. In the seat of my brow I must earn bread.[26]

Menzies's vision was not code for rationalising socialist programmes under a liberal banner. The strength of his liberalism stems from a clear understanding that earned private ownership must be the foundation of an economy and that securing social licence for a private economy depends on it being able to provide for individuals. His approach did not exist in a vacuum. First, the foundational ideals of the Australian settlement were still present. Second, Menzies's revival occurred in a war-weary nation that was toying with socialism under the Chifley government and could observe the alternatives of British socialism under the Attlee government and communism throughout the Soviet Union.

A progressive party?

There continues to be a contemporary debate about the type of party Menzies envisioned. A lot of the debate has centred around two quotes. First is Menzies's reflections in his 1967 memoirs, *Afternoon Light*, that "We took the name 'Liberal' because we were determined to be a progressive party, willing to make experiments, in no sense reactionary but believing in the individual, his rights, and his enterprise, and rejecting the socialist panacea". The conclusion many have taken from this quote is that Menzies's party was designed to be a progressive political force.

Second is Menzies's 1974 letters to Heather Henderson, which have recently been published in *Letters to my Daughter*. In April of

1974, he wrote that "the State Executive of the Liberal Party . . . is dominated by what they now call 'Liberals with a small l'—that is to say, Liberals who believe in nothing but who will believe in anything if they think it worth a few votes".[27] In June, he wrote that he founded "a Party which had principles to which I most firmly adhere, principles which have now been completely abandoned by what they call the 'little l' Liberals".[28] The April letter has been used to justify the claim that Menzies was actually a conservative, or at least did not form a progressive political party.

Both analyses are unpersuasive without understanding the use of the words. Menzies was neither a progressive in the modern parlance, nor did he define himself as a conservative. Then the idea of being progressive was more strongly associated with the ideas of social and economic progress. While cyclical, an analysis since Federation shows the term 'progressive' has been used on seventy occasions in election speeches, and is mostly weighted in favour of speeches of leaders of liberal parties in the first half of the twentieth century.[29] A contemporary understanding of progressivism, however, is associated with centre-left progressive political thought and collectivist and identity politics. The clarity of Menzies's vision for his party can be found in his 1965 address to the Federal Council of the Liberal Party. In reflecting on the formation of the party, he argued:

> we must have one Party, full of unity and fire, and we must have a programme, a platform, which will make people understand that we have been thinking in the future . . . and the effect of this forward thinking, this liveliness, this being modern, being prepared to be a little adventurous was the alternative.

In his speech, he answers his own rhetorical question about the basis of the party's political success. He argues that the party's success was based on being "not the conservative party dying hard on the last barricade, but the party of innovations . . . these were evidence of a lively mind and a forward-looking heart" and a party with "modern and progressive ideas".[30] Thus, in defining the party's approach and purpose, he rejects conservatism. Much subsequent debate is, therefore, dedicated to understanding what he meant by "progressive".

His speeches clearly explain that "what makes the whole movement of Liberalism in Australia a powerful force . . . [is that] we want to build in Australia a balanced and strong and progressive and civilized nation in which advances are shared by all sections of the people". He went on to describe a "balanced nation" as:

> a nation in which primary industry and second industry and tertiary industry live side-by-side and achieve a common national purpose. And the moment you say that you stand for a balanced nation, you are stating that whatever is done there must be progress, productivity, advancement for the man on the land, for the man in the factory, for the man on the truck of the railway train. This is a balanced community strong, progressive.[31]

What Menzies understood was that the best way to conserve the Australians society he valued was to define its future, and nothing was more important than an ownership society. An ownership society is anchored in the idea that every individual has a stake in society and its conservation. Nothing reflects this stake better than an individual establishing a family and acquiring homeownership. A home is the ultimate security. Once people own homes, they only have an interest in the conservation of the status quo. Individuals have an instinct for building a home and family because of the security and foundation it provides to then build a life. A family and home is the basis for mutual support, a protection from loneliness and for intergenerational support as people age.

Menzies also understood the shortcomings of political conservatism, which he often characterized as "reactionary" or "Tory". He explained that "change is a fact. It can't be ignored . . . we are all progressives in politics and we say so, repeatedly. There are no people in the whole political arena who are not desperately anxious for change".[32] He accepted that "you have had great leaders of one party who, generations later, might have proved to be leaders of another. This is, of course, inevitable in any changing world or progressive society".[33] He embraced the idea of being conservative around art and architecture. He happily described himself as an "old-fashioned reactionary Tory", when celebrating the Neo-Georgian architectural style at the opening of the Liberal Party's Federal headquarters,[34] and as "a reactionary traditionalist" at an Adelaide art gallery opening,[35] to chortles of laughter.

His ridiculing of reactionary politics was not just reserved for those on the far right, but also for those on the far left, condemning "a few hopelessly reactionary people, like socialists and communists, (the most reactionary people in the country) who want to whip up something about class distinction",[36] and "The truth is that they are the reactionaries in politics in this country. They are living in the past, they are living on a little stock of ideas".[37] Menzies saw reactionary forces as those who sought to divide society into the haves and have-nots, capital and labour, inherited privilege and working poor. He understood the future of our nation was built on a society of opportunity and ownership so that everyone had a stake in the nation's success.

The idea of conservatism as a political force has never had much currency in Australia. An analysis of the use of the word in election speeches by leaders finds only fifteen mentions, and often by Labor leaders. That is because the word 'conservative' was used by Australians around the middle of the twentieth century to refer to reactionaries, and is now more strongly associated with the modern political conservativism that is interested in conformity. The journalist Alan Reid referred to Menzies as a "cautious reformer",[38] who was Burkean in the value he placed on institutions and culture and the need to conserve them as part of the social fabric that brought people together through a form of nationhood, and also because these institutions and culture are designed to defend individuals.

Menzies did not create a progressive party in the contemporary sense of progressive. Nor did he create an ideologically conservative party. He created a Liberal Party that was for the progress of all.

The very idea of defining yourself as a conservative in Australia is a relatively recent trend. In particular, the thought that 'conservative' is interchangeable with being 'liberal' is a very recent development. Until the mid-twentieth century, 'conservatism' was understood to be interchangeable with 'reactionary'. It goes to the heart of why Menzies referred to his new party as 'progressive'. Although the modern usage is generally associated with a left-wing approach to culture and institutions, it seems pretty clear that when Menzies referred to 'progressive', it was not only a rejection of conservative-reactionary politics, but also a focus on national economic and social progress.

The emergence of a conservative political ideology is normally a mishmash of two underpinning pillars of Australian liberalism—

cultural and institutional conservation—merged with two pillars that really aren't part of Australian liberalism—economic nationalism and social moralism. The first two principles aren't overly unique even to Australian liberalism, and are often held by social democratic parties as well. The last two are what lead ideological conservatives to narrow their constituency.

The spirit of national unity that comes from cultural and institutional conservation is evident in Menzies's 1954 speech to the Adelaide Institute of Management:

> We are all Australians, of common race, language, literature, traditions, and religious faith. With few exceptions, we began life with no advantages of wealth or social position. We believe in the equal rule of law and in the dignity of self-government. We are British through and through. We are for the Crown. We are the Queen's men and women. We all believe in progress, in development, in social justice. What a wealth of agreement we have here! We disagree; of course; about socialism; about the limits of functions of government; about financial policies; about the principles of administration; about foreign policy; about many things. But the truth remains that, if we concentrate on our differences and forget our unities, politics will sound and be-like civil war. The one thing that the bitter and narrow partisans forget is that continuity of national security and growth requires, on great matters, a certain continuity of policy. We secure that by remembering our unities; we destroy it by thinking only of our differences. I, as you may have gathered, am a Liberal, with deep and strong convictions. My opponents, including men of great ability, are Socialists. So let the fight go on. But whoever wins between us, may Australia win always".[41]

The task before a Liberal Party in the liberal mould was to conserve our institutions and cultural inheritance—but it was not enough. As Bramston writes of Menzies, he understood the critical role of leaders and that political parties "need an animating vision for the nation they seek to lead. Leaders must be able to articulate to their supporters, and to the voters, how their principles inform their policies. A clear philosophy gives a party coherence and guidance. It offers a reason to keep the faith".[39] He continues, "Menzies understood that politics is about persuasion, and that effective advocacy is based on a mix of logic, reason, and emotion".[40] The best means of achieving such a vision is to enable Australians to see their success through the success of the country. Whether people can be animated to do so is limited, however, by whether they believe they have an equal place at the table—noble in its egalitarianism, democratic in its ownership and responsibility, and united in its mutually reinforcing individual and national advancement.

Menzies, individuals and homeownership

In many ways, what he saw in Australia was a literal commonwealth. He understood that Australia is a nation where private ownership should be as democratic as possible and didn't foster class-based restrictions or barriers to individual economic advancement. Such common wealth has to be developed through the efficiency of free enterprise to improve the standards of living of individuals and their families as the foundation for national progress. He also understood that the strength of a nation comes from having a society of individuals; not a society divided by class-based ownership of property. Every individual had opportunity. Every individual had ownership. Every individual had an interest in conserving the institutions and culture that underpinned our society because each individual had an investment, and then had the security to contribute to economic and social progress anchored around dignity, a home, and family:

Australia needs 700,000 new homes in the next ten years. This calls for a productive effort in housing almost twice as great as before the war. Our people are entitled to good homes at a cost which bears some proper relation to their earnings. Above all, they want a chance to become the owners of their homes . . . [and] we believe that the encouragement of homeownership is of vital importance, and that Commonwealth financial assistance must be directed primarily to that end.[42]

While the ideal of Commonwealth power being used to promote homeownership may seem inconsistent with a libertarian vision to leave the market economy to resolve this through price signals, it reflected the reality of the post-War era, which followed on from years in which the lives of many veterans and their families were abruptly displaced. It was an ideal that fitted as part of the reconstruction effort of a liberal society.

Menzies's vision valued homeownership. It was also the path to developing a constituency for liberalism itself, because private property and ownership provide individuals with security or "a 'stake in the country' . . . [through] responsibility for homes—homes material, homes human and homes spiritual".[43] A home anchors an individual's life—and their sense of duty and self-responsibility—to other people: to family, community, civil society, and the nation.

Menzies's political achievement, in bridging the diversity of ideas that make up Australian liberalism, is one of the most important moments in liberalism's development into an effective political force. For those of a conservative disposition, it provided an alternative to social democracy. Yet, the task of uniting a liberal movement is no greater than the challenge of holding it together.

3

The neo-liberal era of equity extraction

Cold war and climate change

Thirty years ago, a generation stood atop a wall that divided the city of Berlin for twenty-eight years. It represented much of the division of the second half of the twentieth century. It wasn't just concrete that fell back to earth. It seemed to be the end of a contest of ideas. American political scientist Francis Fukuyama famously boasted of "the end of history". At the time it seemed right, but the comment should have been seen for the hubris it was. But it also represented the aspiration of a victor after an ideological conflict that brought the world to the precipice of its own destruction. And for the next decade it seemed justified. Liberalism was dominant domestically. Liberal internationalism, which inspires countries to make decisions for the benefit of humanity, would finally have a chance to transcend the realpolitik approach to international relations that focused on countries advancing their own interests.

It took two planes flying into the Twin Towers to reset the focus, but not the narrative. Liberalism was still ascendant—it just found a new opponent motivated by a different mission. And when liberal internationalism reached its peak through the invasion of Afghanistan and Iraq, the United States and its allies thought that they could expedite the development of new democracies modelled on societies that took centuries to mature. The practice never quite met the theory.

By the end of the decade, liberal internationalism once again confronted reality at the Copenhagen climate conference. The Conference was supposed to be a united international effort to cut global greenhouse gas emissions, and demonstrate that countries could look beyond their self-interest. Ordinarily, such meetings are attended by the relevant ministers responsible for signing off such a deal. To give the moment its gravity, leaders from American President Barack Obama to Chinese Premier Wen Jiabao, German Chancellor Angela Merkel and Australian Prime Minister Kevin Rudd flew into the Danish capital so they could ink their name personally on the Copenhagen Accord. But instead of the negotiation of an agreement to succeed the Kyoto Protocol, which bound countries to cut emissions, the meeting could only produce a commitment to further discussion. Liberal internationalism got a cold hard real[ity]politik check. Countries were never going to trade away their sovereignty for higher energy prices, which would stifle economic growth and jobs following the global financial crisis, in order to address a distant global environmental threat.

The consequences of the economic crisis continue to linger. Few governments have succeeded in regaining control of their balance sheets. Public debt continues to grow in most nations. Private debt has followed suit. The era of privatisation in Australia is largely over.

Capital has been extracted, and few new investments have been made to replace it. Monetary policy is exhausted with interest rates near zero. Any further steps risk the debasing of our currency itself. Australia isn't alone. Our strength going into the crisis has meant we are still in a stronger situation than other nations. Public debt is still low as a share of gross domestic product (GDP). It took us longer to get near zero in interest rates than it took in comparable countries. Where we excel is in private debt, but we are an ownership society backed up with assets—at least for now.

This may seem like a dismal picture. But the grass is always greener. The tradeoff is that most Australians have jobs, live longer, enjoy a healthy environment that is getting better, and have greater access to life-extending and life-saving treatment and medicines. For all our anxiety, we are living as good a life as human beings ever have. His motivations were hollow, simplistic, and partisan, but Kevin Rudd, was at least partly right when he followed Fukuyama's boastfulness. He claimed neo-liberalism caused the global financial crisis.[1] A more accurate assessment, however, would be that the global financial crisis was the end of the neo-liberal era.

The neo-liberal era

The neo-liberal era was a reaction to the post-War consensus of public ownership, domestic constraint on competition, and trade protectionism associated with the twentieth-century English economist, John Maynard Keynes.

Throughout much of the twentieth century, governments promoted differing forms of state-owned corporatism in many public utilities, as well as state-sponsored corporatism through industry protection.

In the public sector, government agencies had become bloated and corporations were rarely exposed to competition. In practice, they simply accumulated capital and equity for little output, plagued by cultures of inefficiency.

Not that protected private industries were much better. They ensured that capital that could have been used for future investments, innovation, and growth was consumed for non-productive purposes. The neo-liberal ideal was to extract that equity, use the power of the market to increase jobs and opportunity, and promote efficiency through competition.

Keynesian failures reached their high point under the banner of President Jimmy Carter's declaration of 'malaise' over the American economy and Prime Minister James Callaghan's 'winter of discontent' that led entire industries within the British economy to go on strike, and 1970s economic 'stagflation' around the developed world, as well as high unemployment complemented by inflation. In their economic history of the period, *The Commanding Heights: The Battle for the World Economy*, international economists Daniel Yergin and Joseph Stanislaw outlined:

> by the early 1970s, inflationary pressures were becoming more pronounced and visible. The tools government has used to muddle through—to sustain consumer demand, to match inflation with wage increases were now inadequate. Keynesian demand management assumed that low unemployment and a low, managed rate of inflation was a sustainable combination. That proved wrong.[2]

It led to centre-right parties rediscovering classical liberal thought. Whereas, classical liberalism was an evolution of broadly continuous events and thought reflecting the development of economies and society that was disrupted by the First World War, neo-liberalism was the reapplication of classical liberal ideas to the architecture of a late twentieth-century economic and social context.

And in the process the practical application of liberalism changed. Liberalism became less focused on empowering the individual, and became more focused on advancing freedom—freeing up individuals, enterprise, capital, mobility, and technology. The pendulum swung, and for the most part the economists took over in understanding liberalism's priorities. There were good reasons why this was the case. Controls over the economy were stifling economic advancement, as well as empowering governments to control people in ways that affected their basic freedoms to contract their labour and earn a livelihood to support themselves and their families. The trade-off was that the focus on the extraction of capital aligned the immediate objectives of liberalism more closely with efficiency.

Equity extraction

The thirty-year neo-liberal era can probably be best identified as an era of equity extraction. Extracting equity from a corporation is a straightforward exercise of freeing up economic capital to be used for another purpose. But the era of equity extraction wasn't just about economic capital. It also involved the extraction of social solidarity between people and governments that put individualist freedom ahead of social, political, and economic structures designed to advance the individual.

Neo-liberalism was actually quite radical and principally sought to unpack the economic structures of the late twentieth century and reorganize them to focus on freedom of enterprise, and away from the Keynesian era. Neo-liberalism was aided by the economic and technological integration of globalisation that also followed the end of the Cold War, which enlarged the freedom for everyone: the freedom of capital and commerce, communications, and talent.

It worked. Capital was once in drought. Today the world is flooded (though the Covid-19 pandemic may test the extent of the flood). The inflation dragon has been slain. And the extraction of capital has enabled new industries to burgeon and to create new wealth. Technology has liberated industries by saving costs and time, allowing new wealth to be repurposed to stimulate economic growth and job opportunities. This is a global story.

Rates of extreme poverty have been slashed. According to researchers at the University of Oxford, in 1820 approximately 89.15% of the world's population lived in extreme poverty (where such poverty constitutes living on less than USD$1.90 a day). By 1999, it was 28.63%, with the biggest drops occurring after the Second World War. It is now less than 10% and still falling.[3]

Capital is not the only thing that has been extracted. The rising global population and living standards have resulted in equity extraction from the environment. There's a greater demand for energy and resources than ever before.

There has been a recent reinvigoration of population theory associated with the Reverend Thomas Robert Malthus, as laid out in his 1798 *An Essay on the Principle of Population*. The theory is that there is a limit to population growth that the world can sustain. This became popular again with the 1972 publication of *The Limits to Growth*, in which MIT academics used simulations to predict that demands on the earth's resources would peak around the 2020s, in response to demand from population growth. It hasn't proven accurate. This is because the MIT academics didn't foresee technological innovation. Thus, growth persists.

Environmental groups argue that we are consuming the world's renewable resources at a rate equivalent to the needs of 1.7 earths, and that this will almost double again by 2050.[4] This is a relatively simplistic assessment. Poverty can be equally deleterious to the environment. While people living in poverty may not emit as much carbon dioxide from the burning of coal, the burning of biomass is common in developing countries as a source of heat and cooking, and is often done in closed environments leading to the release of carbon dioxide, concurrently harming people's health. Poverty has its own environmental footprint. Simon Kuznet, an economist writing in the 1950s, hypothesised that economies dependent on primary industries start with low inequality and progressively become more unequal as they industrialise, until an inflection point as economies become more service-orientated. Kuznet's curve was later adapted to demonstrate a similar trend between environmental degradation and GDP. This showed that as GDP rose, it would lead to higher environmental degradation, until it declined as people expected conservation and tighter regulation. Studies have challenged the environmental Kuznet curve's validity, on the basis that regulatory and technological innovation can enable an economy's environmental footprint to shrink faster than improvements in GDP.[5]

There are too many metrics to assess the total environmental impact of people's behaviour. Logic requires that demand will inevitably increase with rising global populations as well as incomes. However, technology is reducing aspects of consumption from transitions in energy demand from non-renewable resources to those with lower emissions footprints, such as solar, nuclear, and hydroelectric power.

We have lived through an era of technology equity extraction. Technology is ensuring greater efficiency in many products. A simple iPhone now includes functions that would once have required enough equipment to fill a room. It does so at a fraction of the price, leading to a great democratisation through efficiency. The list is nearly endless: books, e-readers, newspapers, still and video cameras, dictionaries, scanners, bank facilities, maps, video game consoles, cassette players, radios, and computers, among many other technologies that have been completely or partly superseded.[6]

In *More from Less: The surprising story of how we learned to prosper using fewer resources—and what happens next*, Andrew McAfee, argues that "tech progress, capitalism, public awareness, and responsive government [are] the 'four horsemen of the optimist'".[7] His argument is that the power of these four influences ultimately drives efficiency and productivity to address the consequences of seemingly finite resources. He is even prepared to make bets about the general direction of the consumption of certain natural resources over the next decade, and the likely decline in consumption while the population rises. He attributes this not only to a reduction in the resources needed to produce output, but also a decline in complimentary inputs and byproducts:

> Between 1982 and 2015 over 45 million acres—an amount of cropland equal in size to the state of Washington—was returned to nature. Over the same time potassium, phosphate, and nitrogen (the three main fertilizers) all saw declines in absolute use. Meanwhile, the total tonnage of crops produced in the country increased by more than 35 percent. As impressive as this is, it's dwarfed by the productivity improvements of American dairy cows. In 1950 we got 117 billion pounds of milk from 22 million cows. In 2015 we got 209 billion pounds from just 9 million animals. The average milk cow's productivity thus improved by over 330 percent during that time.[8]

And instead of embracing a Malthusian pessimism about the risks of population growth, he embraces the challenge and opportunity that flows from the compounding influence of technology:

> As today's poor get richer, they'll consume more, but they'll also consume much differently from earlier generations. They won't read physical newspapers and magazines. They'll get a great deal of their power from renewables and (one hopes) nuclear because these energy sources will be the cheapest. They'll live in cities . . . [and] in fact, they already are. They'll be less likely to own cars because a variety of transportation options will be only a few taps away. Most important, they'll come up with ideas that keep the growth going, and that benefit both humanity and the planet we live on. Predicting exactly how technological progress will unfold is much like predicting the weather: feasible in the short term, but impossible over a longer time. Great uncertainty and complexity prevent precise forecasts about, for example, the computing devices we'll be using thirty years from now or the dominant types of artificial intelligence in 2050 and beyond.[9]

No one knows what the future will hold. But past trends show we are likely to continue to decrease demand on the world's resources for consumption aligned with population growth as ingenious technology extracts the equity of resources.

While there have been incredible economic and social gains from technology, it has also extracted the equity out of our private and family lives by blurring the beginning and end of work. Global economic integration has led to the extraction of wage growth in developed countries while increasing wages in developing countries. Products and services that were once the domain of domestic markets have integrated into global supply chains, and the benefits of scale have led to relocations of labour. Today, rich countries can only extract premiums when they compete in terms of quality and skills.

The consequences of shifts in employment now raise serious questions for many average citizens who have simple expectations of the economic system—security of employment and wages—which enable them to build a family, home, and life. So the economic impact on ordinary citizens also eats into the equity of our democracy. The Australian National University's Australian Election Study collects data on the electoral attitude of Australians since 1967. The long-term data is not encouraging. Since the end of the 1980s, and particularly since 2007, the trend has been a progressive decline in satisfaction in democracy and a belief that "people in government look after themselves . . . [and] a few big interests".[10] In part, this reflects aspirations associated with electoral cycles.

This raises questions about whether our democracy and economic system still work for individuals, and not just capital and power. In his book, *Ruling the Void: the Hollowing Western Democracy*, Peter Mair identifies realignments of politics in the twentieth century that have led to a disconnect between citizens and their political system. The decline in participation with political parties is most stark: "party organizations, however defined, are now less well rooted within wider society; and second, they are also now more strongly orientated towards government and the State".[11] This has resulted in increasing centralisation of power away from decentralised civil society to the centralised state. He argues that state actors now see themselves as the solution, and that they co-op civil society as pseudo-state actors to achieve state outcomes.

Erosion of confidence in politics

The Museum of Australian Democracy's poll on trust and democracy in Australia found satisfaction with our democracy was directly correlated with improvements in income distributions. Slightly more than a third of those earning less than $50,000 were dissatisfied with our democracy, compared with only 11% of those earning more than $200,000. In the latter category, 52% were either satisfied or very satisfied.[12]

Comparably, the Edelman Trust Barometer has assessed public sentiment toward different institutions since the turn of the millennium. This includes government, non-government organizations, media, and business. Unsurprisingly, data varies for each country, but trust in media and government sits below 50% for most of the surveyed countries,* while trust in businesses and non-government organizations sits slightly above this threshold.[13]

Oddly, the countries that dominate the top four positions on trust in government are China (86%), the United Arab Emirates (82%), Indonesia (75%), and India (74%). All of these are assessed harshly on Transparency International's corruption index (apart from the UAE, which ranks 23 out of 180 countries), which converts each country's trust index to a corruption score.[14]

It's hard to draw clear conclusions from the diversity of global data. Different countries' data reflects their differing stages of development and unique conditions. The overall picture is that trust is high where differing political, economic, and social institutions across a range of metrics are perceived by the community to be working for their own individuals' progress.[15] And that is the challenge our society

---

*   2019 data

faces today. There is a genuine question about whether Australia, and other Western liberal democracies, are still working for their citizens: whether work still brings reward; whether government still reflects citizens' will; and whether people can seek out opportunity and secure reward for their effort. The neo-liberal era has blurred the lines that were once clear.

So what has changed? There are the predictable culprits we all like to blame. Social media has reduced our attention span. Confirmation bias is now rife in our self-selected media consumption. The rapidly increasing wealth of the 1% is making the rich richer, and the poor poorer. The increasing economic power of China is readjusting the gravitational force of geopolitical power from the Atlantic to the Pacific. And climate change seems to be responsible for everything ranging from cricket no longer being able to be played during summer days,[16] through to the cost of producing beer.[17]

None should be dismissed. Each have validity. But none is necessarily central to changing people's lived experience and the ongoing social licence of liberalism. We may think that social media and confirmation bias have destroyed the shared experience we enjoyed when we all consumed the same type of news and information, but the twentieth century was the aberration.

Since the invention of the Gutenberg press, the diversity of ideas flourished, and often through reflected confirmation bias. The great liberal thinker and republican, Thomas Paine, like so many others, was an obsessive pamphleteer whose political opinions were circulated to the masses, and found a home amongst democratic readers.

Advances in technology have tested the foundations of many societies, all of which have had to adapt to forces that are largely beyond their control. Some, such as North Korea, have used the new technology to shut the rest of the world out. Others, such as China, have used it to embrace an alternative reality, through the development of their own internet.

After thirty settled years, we have returned to an era of contestability, as the rise of China and the influence of Russia have demonstrated, through the alternatives for economic and social progress that they offer. Russia's president, Vladimir Putin, has even gone so far as to declare "the liberal idea has become obsolete. It has come into conflict with the overwhelming majority of the population".[18] Putin's first sentence grabbed the headlines and was brandished across the front page of the *Financial Times*. But it is the insight of the second sentence that reflects the challenge that liberalism faces today.

End of eight-hours social contract

The consequence of equity extraction is that it has touched on all aspects of life. The eight-hours movement started in the mid-nineteenth century to address the exploitation that occurred as a result of the Industrial Revolution. Its primary purpose was to regulate the working day under the banner of "eight hours' labour, eight hours' recreation, eight hours' rest", and to end earlier practices that compelled people to work days of around twelve hours, leaving little time for family or social life. The movement that emerged drew increased attention to the lives of working people through works ranging from Charles Dickens's novels to Karl Marx's *Das Kapital*.

In Australia, the eight-hours movement saw stonemasons building the University of Melbourne down tools and march to the colonial parliament in 1856. Within four years, the eight-hour day had become common place and was celebrated with a public holiday within fourteen years.[19]

The eight-hours movement was not alone. There were many political movements that formed the foundations of Australia's social contract.

At the turn of the twentieth century, it was a social contract between men. Many of the pre-Federation political movements agitated for the establishment of a new social contract between the settlers and the colonial authorities as the foundation for the character and expectation of the emerging Australia. The Eureka Rebellion fought against an over-extension of colonial power against the rights of men in 1854. The influence of the Chartist movement in England that focused on universal suffrage and electoral franchise found its way to the antipodes and spoke to colonial expectations of democracy. This, coupled with free trade and the aspiration for colonial self-determination, provided the ideas that would become the foundation for delivering the social contract that future generations of Australians would come to expect.

As outlined in Chapter 2, the British professor of law, Hugh Collins, rejects the idea that social contract theory is embraced in Australia because of the absence of a culture anchored in "the notion of natural rights which was central in both the American and the French revolutions".[20] Collins's observation is correct. Australia lacks a tradition of a rights-based culture. But that does not mean Australia is hostile to the concept of a social contract. Like everything we do, we have our own interpretation of it. The culmination of social contract theory, natural rights, and government by consent transferred from Europe to the Australian continent. European settlers then had a politically blank canvas to develop their practical application afresh and absent the historical legacy of the old world.

The appeal lies in the way that the liberal tradition explains how a social contract functions as the foundation for the relationship between the governed and those that govern. The theoretical ideas of the social contract were authored by thinkers like English philosophers, Thomas Hobbes and John Locke, and their Swiss counterpart, Jean-Jacques Rosseau and his insights into the French Revolution. Hobbes conceived of the social contract as a transfer of natural rights from the individual for the sake of collective security through mutual interest with their peers for safety and peace. Locke also recognised that individuals transferred some of their natural rights to governments, in order to ensure a stable climate for the preservation of liberty from an overbearing state, including the protection of property. Rosseau understood that the social contract was necessary because individuals relied on different forms of mutual dependence for their own unaided needs and that government operates on a form of consent from the governed.

The concept of social contract is a claim about the legitimacy of the state and the citizen's obligation to accept the state's authority. As David Kemp argues in *The Land of Dreams*:

> The role of government was to protect these rights, and their effective protection constituted the most important terms of the social contract between government and its citizens. The contract involved such terms as the protection of the liberty of the subjects, and of their property— terms that went to the heart of the private interests of the most powerful subjects and, they argued, to the public interest as well.[21]

Kemp argues that Mill's analysis of property distribution in Britain has a profound significance in the Australian colonies. It informed understandings of the opportunity and promise of our continent and the social contract:

> Mill argued that at the heart of the social problems of poverty and degradation in Britain was the extreme inequity in the distribution of wealth, combined with an excessive population growth relative to resources. The distribution of wealth had not come about as a result of the activities of individual accumulating property under a framework of just laws.[22]

Kemp's analysis follows from Mill's criticism of socialism, where he affirmed the importance of the democratisation of property for achieving shared economic progress, and also that the allocation and rents enjoyed from property must be coupled with an obligation for it to be earned:

> The principle of private property has never yet had a fair trial in any country . . . they have purposely fostered inequalities, and prevented all from starting fair in the race . . . if the tendency of legislation had been to favour the diffusion, instead of the concentration of wealth— to encourage the subdivision of the large masses, instead of striving to keep them together ; the principle of individual property would have been found to have no necessary connection with the physical and social evils which almost all Socialist writers assume to be inseparable from it. Private property, in every defence made of it, is supposed to mean the guarantee to individuals of the fruits of their own labour and abstinence. The guarantee to them of the fruits of the labour and abstinence of others, transmitted to them without any merit or exertion of their own, is not of the essence of the institution.[23]

Mill's focus needs to be contextualised to its time in Europe, when property was held as a result "not of just partition, or acquisition by industry, but of conquest and violence".[24] What Mill argued was that the socialist critique of property rights flowed directly from its unjust acquisition and then earned passive income from the labour of others without their own effort; meaning there was not even any investment—unless you classify conquest and the use of violence to secure property effort! In contrast, property secured in an open economy through individual effort enjoys social licence as reward for the "fruits of their own labour".

There was an awareness of the potential that bountiful land offered for the economic opportunity of the Australian colonies. The *1909 Year Book* of the Commonwealth Bureau of Census and Statistics, published an authoritative assessment of land tenure and settlement in the early colonies, identifies "the various forms of land tenure which have been adopted with a view to securing the settlement of a large and sparsely populated country like Australia . . . [had] an important and immediate bearing upon the welfare of the community".[25] Assessing tenure colony by colony, it describes the "first grants of land made in New South Wales":

> The first instructions, issued on the 25th April, 1787, authorised the Governor to make grants only to liberated prisoners. The grant was to be free from all taxes, rents, fees, and other acknowledgments for the space of ten years, after which period an annual quit-rent of sixpence for thirty acres was payable; for each unmarried male the grant was not to exceed thirty acres; in case of a married man twenty' acres more was allowed, and a further quantity of ten acres for each child living with his or her parents at the time of making such grant.[26]

And:

> in 1789, the privilege of obtaining grants was extended to free immigrants and to such of the men belonging to the detachment of marines serving in New South Wales— which then included the whole of the eastern part

of Australia—as were desirous of settling in the colony; the maximum grant was not to exceed 100 acres . . . In many cases these grants were made conditional upon a certain proportion of the land being cultivated, or upon certain services being regularly performed. [27]

Land-anchored hereditary titles were not recreated; there was no Duke of Port Jackson. Land allocation was deliberately controlled, with ceilings on the generosity of the Crown. Such allocations need to be put in the context of the small European population and the vastness of the continent, as well as the colony's needs: an obligation had to be imposed to ensure the land was used to generate income through cultivation, in order to meet the colony's need for food supply. But a social contract tied to property ownership had begun.

There is no agreed definition of the social contract. Consistent themes include the agreement citizens make with each other, and between themselves and their government as a foundation for the government's legitimacy, the citizen's freedom, and society's order. After Hobbes, Locke, and Rosseau, the concept of the social contract has continued to evolve. The influential twentieth-century American liberal philosopher, John Rawls, argued that the legitimacy of the state depends upon the ongoing dialogue of justice to advance society. He maintains that this is achieved because each of us accepts the need for justice when we approach the problem from the perspective of a "veil of ignorance" as to the circumstances into which we happen to be born.

It links the very basis of the legitimacy of the government to respect for the individual's civil rights, while also providing the pathway for individuals to realise their freedom to pursue their own life. The strength of the social contract is the way in which it links social obligation to the government's acceptance that individuals must be able to pursue their private interests, which is in turn reinforced by the individual's acceptance that individual flourishing requires acceptance of the legitimacy of the state.

Kemp demonstrates that social contract has been part of Australian life since European settlement. He explains that acceptance of social contract theory by the early colonists did not mean that they simply espoused philosophical ideas, but "a statement about the way the world operated, and British colonial experience would confirm its validity . . . the idea of the social contract touched on an aspect of the way societies worked that was very real and could not be ignored".[28] Peter Lalor's later liberal motivation at the Eureka Rebellion was motivated, according to Kemp, by a perception of the "breaking of the social contract" and "that the rule of the majority had to be checked in the interests of protecting minorities".[29] The co-opting of Chartism by colonial Australians was also a reflection of an evolving social contract about the equal dignity of citizens and their compact with the state.

Thus, social contract theory has never been absent from the Australian story. In many ways, it has dominated the ongoing dialogue of our politics: how best to govern a society balances just, moral and utilitarian outcomes to maximum private interests, while respecting the freedom of individuals and minorities.

Critical to any understanding of the social contract is to understand that it evolves. It is not a static statement about the relationship between citizens and government, but a discussion about the basis of the government's ongoing legitimacy depending upon individuals accepting that the government continues to be committed to ensuring individuals can achieve their aspirations. This is particularly true in

Australia, which was not born of revolution, but which does have a flexible constitutional framework that defines the boundaries of our democracy without predetermining our national destination. Australia's social contract is a perpetual evolution.

In his landmark analysis of the tumultuous 1980s, the nation's biographer and journalist, Paul Kelly, wrote of the end of the "Australian settlement". The settlement was his way of capturing the foundational ideas accepted across all political divides, and which led to the development of a social contract for the new nation and its people after Federation:

> The generation after Federation in 1901 turned an emerging national consensus into new laws and institutions. This was the Australian settlement . . . the nation was founded not in war, revolution or national assertion, but by practical men striving for income, justice, employment and security . . . summarised under five hearings—White Australia [which had both racial and cultural dimensions], Industry Protection, Wage Arbitration, State Paternalism, and Imperial Benevolence.[30]

Despite progress on gender, the young nation didn't extend the spirit of inclusion to those from a non-Anglo background. The social contract ultimately sits in a context, and it can only exist in a society that is anchored on membership of a defined community. At that time, the defined community was much broader as part of the British Empire. While we look at the operation of the White Australia Policy today as a stain on the nation's past, to the extent there was an Australian identity at the turn of the twentieth century, it was exclusionary and connected back to settlement from the United Kingdom. As that identity developed throughout the century, it broadened and absorbed waves of migration from post-War Europe, and later migration from Asian nations and the rest of the world. At all times, the social contract has evolved to reflect the ambition of the people for the role of government to deliver for them.

The First and Second World Wars displaced any real discussion of the social contract for survival, particularly during the war in the Pacific. The Great Depression tested the very limits of Australians' economic expectations, and the extent to which these could be curtailed. Through the swift action of the Lyons government, which preferred prudence over stimulus, there was a halt to spending and Australia's economic misfortune was reversed much faster than comparable nations.

In Australian political history, Menzies best demonstrates the commitment to honouring the social contract. He sought to maintain a liberal democracy that promoted economic and social progress through the realisation of the aspirations of Australians. This was achieved through opportunities for employment, respect for individuality, and a commitment to homeownership. And it was achieved against the backdrop of a government that sought to define a vision for a prosperous, secure, and united Australia. Menzies articulated all of this best in his memoir, *The Measure of the Years*, when he wrote that "the prime duty of government is to encourage enterprise, to provide a climate favorable to its growth, to remember that it is the individual whose energies produce progress, and that all social benefits derive from his efforts".[31]

As the principles of a social contract became settled, the majority of Australians did not experience injustices and inequities. So too, other injustices and inequities were progressively addressed. Notably, this included the Holt government's leadership in passing the 1967 referendum to count Aboriginal people in the census, and the beginning of the end of the white Australia policy. John Gorton's

1973 motion in the federal parliament to legalise homosexuality commenced a series of State and federal reforms that ultimately led to sexual activity between consenting adults being tolerated, and then their unions being legally recognised in 2017.

At least in legal terms, almost all Australians have an equal legal stake in our society. Legal equality alone is not sufficient for the ongoing legitimacy of a liberal democracy. This has been built on a social contract of live-and-let live mutual respect. The task before us today is how to renew its relevance by addressing contemporary challenges in order to meet the full breadth of Australian society's expectations. That's the hard part.

A just and equal society

Political ideologies prioritise a single principle. As we discussed in Chapter 1, liberalism is anchored in the empowerment of individuals and principles such as respect for the equality and dignity of the individual, their freedom to take responsibility in pursuit of their life and enterprise, and the necessity of a liberal understanding of justice. For liberalism to thrive, it requires all individuals to be in full flight.

What has changed in the neo-liberal era is not just that freedom has been prioritised but that it has been prioritised in a way that has failed to give weight to the liberal idea of justice, which is also necessary to maintain the social licence for liberalism. And as neo-liberalism has reached its limits, particularly after the global financial crisis, we need to rediscover the place of justice within a liberal worldview. Only with a renewed liberal outlook that leaves neo-liberalism behind can we address contemporary challenges and rebuild liberalism's social licence.

One of the great challenges of any society is to define the concept of justice. It is politically amorphous. Much is driven by the cultural context in which it operates. All forms of justice ultimately rest on a balance between people. There is no single conception of justice running throughout liberal thinking. Despite modern misconceptions, social justice is not foreign to liberalism. But equally, liberalism does not regard justice as an outright justification for suppressing the freedom and property of others. As Adam Smith argues in *The Theory of Moral Sentiments*:

> The laws of all civilised nations oblige parents to maintain their children, and children to maintain their parents, and impose upon men many other duties of beneficence. The civil magistrate is entrusted with the power not only of preserving the public peace by restraining injustice, but of promoting the prosperity of the commonwealth, by establishing good discipline and by discouraging every sort of vice and impropriety; he may prescribe rules, therefore which not only prohibit mutual injuries among fellow-citizens, but command mutual good offices to a certain degree.[32]

Critically, what Smith observes in his discussion on justice is that a sense of commonwealth and mutual obligation sits at the heart of any flourishing society. He writes:

> all the members of human society stand in need of each other's assistance, and are likewise exposed to mutual injuries. Where the necessary assistance is reciprocally afforded from love, from gratitude, from friendship, and esteem, the society flourishes and is happy. All the different members of it bound together by the agreeable bands of love and affection, and are, as it were, drawn to one common centre of mutual good offices.[33]

Furthermore, he argues that a society can survive on the simple basis of "utility" even if it is "less happy and agreeable", but cannot:

subsist among those who are at all times ready to hurt and injure one another. The moment that injury begins, the moment that mutual resentment and animosity take place, all the bands of it are broke asunder, and the different members of which it consisted are, as it were, dissipated and scattered abroad by the violence and opposition of their discordant affections.[34]

In Smith's view, justice is about the relationship that comes from mutuality. But the critical underpinning is that harmony is central to the social legitimacy of justice in society. While individuals can disagree, if they have a continuing interest in the way their interests are advanced by the existing order, then the disagreement will never escalate to compromise the legitimacy of the order that risked or tolerated the creation of the injustice. Society struggles when resentment becomes so great that differing parties no longer share a common interest.

The role of justice is critical to the legitimacy of the social contract that sits within a society because it anchors expectations between the individuals and the state, both in the protection of the individuals' liberty and the necessary trade-offs to conserve and advance it. Justice for mutuality has two components. The first is between people in the moment: how people relate to each other at the same time. That sense of mutuality informs discussions around the development of social welfare systems and the terms of contracts. The second is over time: what we inherit, and how we relate to those that come after us in a way that extends to equal opportunity, the health of the environment, and ideas of the connection between the social contract and intergenerational justice best articulated by British Whig parliamentarian and philosopher, Edmund Burke, in his *Reflections on the Revolution in France*, that:

Society is indeed a contract . . The state . . is . . a partnership not only between those who are living, but between those who are living, those who are dead, and those who are to be born. Each contract of each particular state is but a clause in the great primeval contract of eternal society.[35]

These ideas of mutuality are represented in both equality of opportunity and intergenerational justice. F. A. Hayek understood the concerns of equality of opportunity. In *Law, Legislation and Liberty*, he warned against using the mirage of social justice as simply a "struggle", which "becomes in practice a struggle for power of organized interests in which arguments of justice serve merely as pretexts".[36] Hayek's observations are salient in liberal thought because he was wary of how social justice could simply become a veil for coercion, and how it can undermine the power of decentralised decision-making that is necessary for markets to be successful. Hayek's concern was not all forms of social justice, but the democratic socialist variety that inevitably lead to the empowerment of centralised authorities to decide what is 'just'.

Hayek appreciates "that the demand for equality of opportunity or equal starting conditions . . . appeals to, and has been supported by, many who in general favour the free market order". What he rejects, however, is the idea that equality of opportunity amounts to equity. To accept this, he believes, would ultimately empower a government to disregard individuality and reward for effort for the sake of creating a perfectly equal society.

This is a view shared by Milton Friedman. *In Free to Choose: A personal statement*, Friedman argues strongly in favour of an understanding of the divide between equality of opportunity and its symbiotic relationship between liberalism and equality of outcome, which can only be associated with socialism:

> No arbitrary obstacles should prevent people from achieving those positions for which their talents fit them and which their values lead them to seek . . . equality of opportunity, like personal equality, is not inconsistent with liberty; on the contrary, it is an essential component of liberty. If some people are denied access to particular positions in life for which they are qualified simply because of their ethnic background, color, or religion, that is an interference with their right to "Life, Liberty, and the pursuit of Happiness." It denies equality of opportunity and, by the same token, sacrifices the freedom of some for the advantages of others.[37]

There are two fundamental points that both Hayek and Friedman touch upon. The first is that, in a liberal society and economy, individuals should not be disadvantaged or restricted in their participation simply as a consequence of their birth—whether it is race, gender, sexual orientation, or the like. But the obligation then is that only they can be responsible for their own advancement through their own labours. This is the tradition that has led liberals to have a strong commitment to equality before the law. Discrimination by government and law is utterly contradictory to the liberal tradition. It is also why liberals have consistently been strong supporters of (and introduced in the United Kingdom and Australia) universal elementary education. Liberals value education because it enables future generations their equal chance at advancing their own welfare.

The second fundamental point is that a liberal society must not just be open in the sense that individuals do not experience discrimination based on the circumstances of their birth, but that the society must also remain open and not favour one section of society over another. This is one of the most critical differences between conservatism and liberalism. British one-nation conservatism does not seek to remake the nation, despite understanding the privilege that has been afforded to some people through their birth in status and property; nor, for clarity, does liberalism. But one-nation conservatism is relaxed about the maintenance of privilege, so long as those who enjoy it share the benefits. Liberals, however, do not believe in the establishment or maintenance of such privileges. As Austro-British philosopher, Karl Popper, argues in *The Open Society and its enemies*:

> in an open society, many members strive to rise socially, and to take the places of other members. This may lead, for example, to such an important social phenomenon as class struggle.[38]

Liberals fundamentally believe in an open economy and society to provide pathways for individual advancement that remove the abrasiveness needed for any class struggle. An open society and economy facilitates meritocracy through reward for effort and social mobility in return for that effort: that someone can be born poor and low in social standing, work and retire rich, or in higher social standing. The extent of individuals' economic prosperity should depend upon their ingenuity and effort, and their social standing should be reflective of their character and conduct, and the esteem in which they are held by others. It also goes to the heart of why liberals believe in a free market governed by price signals. Any centrally planned economy lacks the information of price signals and replaces it with the uninformed judgement of the central planner. As Hayek wrote in *The Road to Serfdom*:

> In the end somebody's views will have to decide whose interests are more important, and these views must become part of the law of the land. Hence the familiar fact that the more the state 'plans', the more difficult planning becomes for the individual.[39]

Worse, in the absence of price signals, decisions are not made in the economy based on the accumulated knowledge of supply and demand to meet individual want or need, but are open to other considerations. The absence of transparent price signals can only permit other factors to be considered, including relationships and those who have access to decision-makers. It can only lead to corruption by centralised planners. In doing so, central planning artificially creates economic and social structures that diminish both the individual's power in the marketplace and their capacity to compete, and also compromise the capacity of the marketplace to supply what individuals demand.

Similarly, the liberal commitment to an open society and economy is not just about empowering an individual's capacity to be mobile at a fixed time, but also that capacity across the person's life cycle. Whilst there has been the traditional discussion by liberals of the importance of the accumulation, protection, and trade of property rights and the freedom to contract as a form of justice, there hasn't been the extensive reassessment needed as a consequence of people's expanding life cycle. As with the introduction of the publicly funded pension in many countries, it was only designed to support people who on average lived a few short years after their retirement. So too, much of the discussion around property, and the allied discussions of tax, is predicated upon a state of affairs in which people did not expect to enjoy a lengthy retirement. Thus, people expected that their reliance upon income derived from retirement investments, rather than from their own labour, would be more of a temporary than a long term arrangement, and people did not plan for a long retirement.

That world has now changed. People are living long after their working life, and how government protects property (particularly homeownership) has a direct correlation with the opportunity for young people to their lives unshackled by the generations that came before them. Earlier generations will always have an advantage over younger generations resulting from time and the capacity to apply their accumulated skills, labour, and knowledge to the accumulation of capital. Their dependence on the acquiring of capital is also proportionate—young people have time on their side and are less likely to need security. The flipside is that older generations do not have time on their side, and once retired rely on the security that the accumulation of capital can afford. But that does not mean that there are not liberal options for managing this situation.

Government has a responsibility to ensure the property that individuals derive from their labour and their sacrifice is protected. But liberals interested in individual empowerment should not be interested in entrenching any benefit simply because someone is born earlier. One of the most important issues that liberals must confront is the need to ensure that individuals share the tax burden of the nation across the whole of their life cycle and neither secure reward from their stage of life through preferential tax treatment, nor are harmed for the same reason. Keeping economic and social systems open necessitates not creating artificial barriers for younger generations to accumulate property through barriers of taxation or regulation—such as one-off large taxes that favour established interests that already hold capital and continue holding it because of the tax barriers to transactions.

When taxation or regulation is required, it should be done in the least burdensome way possible, such as through a lower-rate subscription tax that favours tradability of property. Similarly, there should be consistency in the application of taxes and regulations across different forms of economic activity. Favourable tax treatment should not be afforded to income derived from the holding or investment of capital that is principally beneficial to established interests. Indeed, such income should be treated consistently with the income derived from labour and the application of skills, which is the principal means of accumulating capital. Intergenerational justice depends on consistent flat tax rates, so individuals can be empowered to move through the stages of their life without barriers that artificially construct disadvantage.

Intergenerational justice

Rawls provides an abstract account of the challenge of intergenerational justice in *A Theory of Justice*. He discusses the "peculiar feature" of the principle underpinning intergenerational justice: "in the course of history no generation gives to the preceding generations, the benefits of whose saving it has received. In following the savings principle, each generation contributes to later generations and receives from its predecessors".[40]

As previously discussed, Rawls assumes that any concrete consideration of justice takes place under a 'veil of ignorance' about the circumstances individuals are born into, so that no one knows what generation they are born into, yet "it is assumed that a generation cares for its immediate descendants, as fathers say care for their sons, a just savings principle, or more accurately, certain limits on such principles, would be acknowledged" and "The just savings principle can be regarded as an understanding between generations to carry their fair share of the burden of realising and preserving a just society".[41]

An intergenerationally just economic system is one that is sufficiently open that it enables present and future generations to pursue their own opportunity, secure their own property and other rewards for effort, and does not overly favour those born into conditions of privilege.

The demographic reality, to be discussed in Chapter 5, is that people are living longer, healthier, and happier lives as a result of medical and technological advancement. And while respect for the accumulation of property should remain, it necessarily leads to a discussion about the obligations of people who live ten, twenty, or thirty years beyond retirement: what they should contribute? What they can expect in return? And who should pay for it? And the same principle also applies to systems of governance. Such systems should also not create an environment of disadvantage for future generations by protecting the interests of those who came before them. In the spirit of an open economy and society in the liberal tradition, and consistent with the social contract, generations should take care of themselves and not leave future generations at unjustified disadvantage. That is why liberals oppose intergenerational economic and environmental debt handed from one generation to the next. Both deprive individuals of future generations of their choices.

4

Liberalism's social licence

The failure of centralised planning

Every political ideology needs constituencies. To enjoy a constituency, it must be seen to the meet the constituency's aspirations. Despite the abject failures of socialism and communism, the ideas that rest behind them continue to enjoy support through organized political movements, technocrats, within the media, and in the halls of the academy. The failure of both can be traced to a shared objective that is flawed, but whose flaws its supporters do not appreciate.

Socialism's pursuit of centralised economic planning and redistribution, and communism's pursuit of a classless society through collective ownership of the means of production, can only achieve their social, political, and economic objectives through the inevitable centralising of all forms of power: economic power, through ownership and redistribution; social and cultural power, to justify conformity; and political power, to constrain criticism of its shortcomings. While power is not strictly binary, in most cases empowerment of centralised authorities to manage issues of equity and empowerment of large corporatised interests for production (whatever the ownership structure) necessitates disempowering individuals from taking responsibility for their own circumstances and denying them the freedom to change such circumstances. Accumulation of centralised power eventually fails for lack of proximity to those whom it serves. Decisions are made for people without consideration of local contexts, deliverability, and suitability. Local cultures and values are ignored.

Individuals are in the best position to decide what is in their own interests. And when that's what is in question, it is rarely clear why someone more distant and with less information is in a better position to decide. The same principles apply with governance. Local councils are in the best position to decide what is in their community's collective interests. And if they get it wrong, the capacity for ordinary citizens is straightforward: the power gap between citizens and elected officials is small, as is the electoral maths to effect change; the physical distance is small, and the time restrictions to prompt action are also modest.

Once elevated to a larger collective, all those gaps expand. The efficacy of state or regional governments is to find the balance between deliverability proportionate to the benefits of scale. But with scale, the power gap, the electoral maths, the geography, time and attitudes that need to be considered expand, and the capacity to affect change declines. At a national level, the gaps are even larger, and need to reflect the diversity of a broader range of opinions reflecting the differing values of communities. That leaves national governments expert at standardisation and relations with other countries, but not in matters that depend on community connection. And the United Nations' universality forces it to be so distant and non-proximate that it can only really pontificate platitudes without any democratic connection that would enjoy universal social licence.

It's the oddity of much modern political dialogue. Many people think it would be better to remove the States for the efficiency of unitary monopoly government. It's a recipe for paralysis. It would lead to individuals with less in common and further from the problems they're trying to solve making decisions. Individuals would have less control. Yet, the exact opposite happens when individuals take responsibility. They know their context. They know their interest. They're in as good a position to decide the consequences of their action as anyone. And, when they fail, they learn and adapt. By comparison, governments can't learn. Only people learn. And any institutional learning or knowledge of a politician, regulator, or bureaucrat can generally survive for their own tenure.

It's a feedback loop like being in a shower. If you're in the shower and the water goes cold, you adjust the cold and hot taps until you get the right temperature. Your capacity to act is immediate, and so is your response. If it requires fixing the hot water service it becomes someone else's responsibility and the practical urgency decreases, knowledge of the ideal temperature declines, and if you have to call someone from a State capital or Canberra to solve the problem you're probably best avoiding the shower for a while. If the problem is the plumbing or the water reservoir, the problem is no longer solvable locally and you're dependent on the action of others. Former American President Ronald Reagan reflected this sentiment in his joke about the Soviet Union:

"I have been collecting stories that I can tell, or prove are being told by the citizens of the Soviet Union among themselves, which display not only a sense of humour but their feeling about their system." Mr. Reagan then told his current favourite, about a Russian who wants to buy a car. A matter of delivery, the man goes to the official agency, puts down his money and is told that he can take delivery of his automobile in exactly 10 years. "Morning or afternoon?" the purchaser asks. "Ten years from now, what difference does it make?" replies the clerk. "Well," says the car-buyer, "the plumber's coming in the morning".[1]

Reagan's joke reflects the folly of centralised planning and decision-making in both government service delivery and the economy. Economically, central planning takes no account of individual need. It can only take account of production leading to waste and inefficiency. That's ultimately the power of price signals. As Hayek explained in *The Road to Serfdom*, "Under competition—and under no other economic order—the price system automatically records all the relevant data. Entrepreneurs, by watching the movement of comparatively few prices, as an engineer watches a few dials, can adjust their activities to those of their fellows".[2] It is a system designed to empower individuals to communicate their needs.

Yet, despite the folly of centralised planning, the temptation persists, and with it the political philosophies that espouse it. Part of socialism's persistence comes from a yearning for a greater sense of redistributive justice motivated to address genuine inequity, as well as utopian ideals to remake the world so as to conform to a socialist idea of an equal society based on outcomes. This pursuit of redistributive justice depends on the reordering of the economy and society to enable the exercise of centralised authority because only the force of government and corporates have the institutional weight to bring about adjustments in the economy or society.

Empowering individuals

The challenge for contemporary liberalism is that the trends are working against it. All political ideologies confront this challenge for their own survival. Liberalism is no different. A power balance favouring decentralised decision-making, in which governments defer to individuals, and the social structures that flow from individuals—family and community—is what gives liberalism its social licence. Liberalism empowers the individual. Through the activity of pursuing their own advancement, people acquire a stake in the community and country beyond themselves. In Australia, the challenge that liberalism faces is that it has drifted away from the core principle of advancing the empowerment of individuals, to focusing obsessively on freedom of the individual as part of the neo-liberal era, and has lost its ballast around a liberal conception of justice. Imbalanced liberalism risks diminishing electoral appeal as it no longer offers the best avenue for many individuals to live the fullness of their aspirations and their lives. The neo-liberal era has increasingly allowed distant, unaccountable, and centralised political power and capital to gain the upper hand.

One of the most basic rules of success in politics is that voters have to be able to see how their lives are lived through the values you project. If they can't see how their life can be lived through what you offer, you have no hope of attracting their support. It isn't because people only vote in their own interest. They don't. But if they can't see how they fit within the vision projected, and that whatever sacrifice is required is also justified, then an alternative vision in which they can see themselves fitting, will always have greater allure.

Today's challenge

The challenge for contemporary politics is that the dividing lines of partisan politics rarely reflect the concerns voters have. Much of the structure of our party politics and even philosophy is built on the dividing lines of yesteryear: capital versus labour. Voters no longer see themselves fitting into visions of a world divided into capital and labour.

In practice, we know that world is long gone. Organized labour continues to decline year-on-year. At its peak, in 1984, three million Australians were union members. Today, union membership rests at 1.5 million—despite substantial population growth in the intervening years.[3] That decline is best evidenced by the number of employed people who are trade union members. In 1979, it was 48.8% of workers. Today, it is 13.6%.[4] Those with the largest share of union membership are industries allied to the public sector—utilities[5] at 32.3%, public administration and safety at 31%, education and training at 33.8%.[6]

Members of a trade union are now eclipsed by the number of people who work for themselves,[7] let alone non-unionised labour, as well as small business owners, and owners of private companies. The pervasiveness of compulsory superannuation has also shifted the dial. The objectives of compulsory superannuation were designed to shift the burden of an ageing population to save for their retirement, as well as giving all Australians a stake in the future prosperity of the nation. That has led ordinary Australians to become decentralised capital holders. Interestingly, the relationship between organised labour and unionised industry superannuation demonstrates they are not just organised labour, but organized, centralised capital too.

Consequently, the dividing line of capital versus labour is really a divide between private versus public,[8] and, arguably, decentralised power versus centralised power.

The tension between centralised interests and those outside has become a common theme of political analysis. Many wrongly conclude this has only been a trend since the seemingly surprising election of Donald Trump and the successful vote for Brexit. In fact, it started some years earlier and has been building during the era of equity extraction.

The new social divide

In 2012, an American political scientist, Charles Murray, wrote *Coming Apart: The State of White America, 1960-2010*. In it, he analysed the underlying trends that are dividing white Americans, in particular, from traditional social structures. Murray recognised the divides between "a new upper class" made up of a "narrow elite" who "have risen to jobs that directly affect the nation's culture, economy, and politics",[9] and a "broad elite" who are "successful and influential within a city or region".[10] They are geographically concentrated in the American equivalent of affluent postcodes that Murray refers to as "SuperZips", and, together, they share an isolation from the rest of their country that involves "spatial, economic, educational, cultural, and, to some degree, political isolation".[11] These new elites no longer have a common shared life with those outside their class—a fact exacerbated by intra-marriage. To aid his argument, he includes a quiz at the end of his book for people to assess the extent that they have lived in the footsteps of a working-class white American.[12]

He compared them to the "new lower class" that "comprises differences that affect the ability of people to live satisfying lives, the ability of communities to function as communities, and the ability of Americans to survive as America".[13] Murray provides insight not just into the problems of economic separation, but also the problems associated with the decline of the social support structures that people rely on. Support structures have collapsed in part because of the absence of economic power, but more particularly as a result of the decline in marriage rates. The data shows that "put plainly, single prime-age males are much less industrious than married ones. Both the decline in marriage and the increased detachment from the labor force . . . cannot be understood without knowing that the interaction exists".[14]

Murray identifies the compounding effects of the absence of the nucleus of mutually dependent and supportive relationships. Such relationships should act as ballast, steadying disadvantaged Americans as they seek to improve their circumstances. The absence of such relationships is coupled with other issues like the rise in disability and increased under-employment rates, all of which Murray connects with the decline in religiosity as one of the cores of "social capital in a community", particularly when economic circumstances limit other avenues for social engagement.[15] Murray's conclusion is that these "trends signify damage to the heart of the American community and the ways in which the great majority of Americans pursue satisfying lives . . . and [the] most exceptional qualities of American culture cannot survive unless they are reversed".[16]

In short, the social fabric that binds individuals and families as the organizing unit of society was in decline, while those empowered through institutions and capital cities thrived and fed on their self-reinforcing success. Traditional political divides are predicated on the idea that it is the concentration of capital that hurts workers. What Murray shows, however, is that it is the compounding weight of influence and wealth that is now putting pressure on fraying social norms and institutions. So it is the weight of influence, rather than just the concentration of capital, that now needs to be addressed.

Murray doesn't sit alone. Six months before Trump's victory, J. D. Vance narrated *Hillbilly Elegy: A memoir of a family and culture in crisis*. It traverses the struggles faced by the Americans he grew up with, in terms of their fight to preserve family life and cultural life. He compares their experiences with the experience of people in Washington DC—a SuperZip metropolis in Murray's thesis. Vance explains that he "grew up in a world where everyone worried about how they'd pay for Christmas"; a world in which "opportunities abound for the wealthy and privileged to show their generosity on the community's poor".[17] It is an America in which, he maintains, "members increasingly occupy two separate worlds".[18]

Murray's analysis was narrowly focused on white America. Following the Brexit referendum, David Goodhart's *The Road to Somewhere: The new tribes shaping British politics* described the challenge within British society. He analyses the challenge in terms of the divergence between the 'anywheres' and the 'somewheres'. Anywheres adhere to a "progressive individualism . . . a worldview for more or less successful individuals who care about society . . . that places a high value on autonomy, mobility and novelty and a much lower value on group identity, traditional and national social contracts . . . see[ing] themselves as citizens of the world".[19] Somewheres "are more socially conservative and communitarian . . . not on the whole highly religious . . . moderately nationalistic . . . uncomfortable about many aspects of cultural and economic change—such as mass immigration . . . [and] want a form of openness that does not disadvantage them".[20] Goodhart's argument is that the attitudes of anywheres have been dominant in decision-making domestically and through international institutions, and the rise of a somewhere populism in reaction is a rebalancing and adjustment.

I got this firsthand in 2016. Prior to my election to the federal parliament, I was asked to participate in a programme sponsored by the British Government's Foreign and Commonwealth Office for leaders in the Asia Pacific. In between being asked to participate, as Australia's Human Rights Commissioner, and participating in the programme, I'd resigned from the Australian Human Rights Commission; got elected to the federal parliament, and the Brexit vote had happened. Like any programme organized by a foreign government, it was designed to represent both the diversity and strength of the sponsoring nation, and to strengthen ties, particularly with other countries that didn't share the kind of deep heritage shared by the United Kingdom and Australia. In the afterglow of the Brexit vote in June, the programme held in September was full of academics and representatives of non-governmental institutions who were still shellshocked and who seemed to feel compelled to apologise for the British people's decision.[21] My personal view on Brexit was always that of a diffident supporter of leave. Diffident largely because it was not my vote, but as a liberal I naturally have an instinctive hostility to the centralisation of power, particularly in a far-off and distant capital of largely unelected officials.

One presenter at the conference spoke explicitly of his personal story of coming to London as a migrant in order to work together to make it an international city. The story was told with scant regard for the wishes and reflections of people born in the United Kingdom. After hearing the presenter's speech, I became aggressive in my support for Brexit. What came across in this presentation was the disconnect between the lives he and his fellow Londoners lived and the much more humble and anchored cultural lives of many Britons, principally those who lived outside the capital. He spoke of jetting between international cities, attending United Nations summits, and participating in NGO forums with opaque and distant humanist objectives. He was essentially disparaging of, and ignorant about, the people and the country that let him in. My response was emotional and akin to the anger that springs when Australian republicans call for an Australian president to show the world that we are a 'grown-up' country. Such responses show a contempt and disregard for our country's history, traditions, and success. But it is hard to think that the average Briton would have reacted any differently. Underpinning this international Londoner's vision was a mixture of contempt and hubris suggestive of some pseudo-feudal right of the well-heeled, educated, and connected internationalists to decide the future of a country with scant concern for the basic economic, cultural, and social concerns of those that foot every part of the country's bill. He was the quintessential 'anywhere'.

The tension between somewheres and anywheres is a reflection of the disconnect between lived experiences. Thus, Goodhart's analysis in terms of an attitudinal and priority gap resonates more with the Australian experience than Murray and Vance's analyses, which focus more on the core organizing units of society. Australia has always been a country of religious and political moderation. Australians have enjoyed the option of education and healthcare services available from religious service providers operating in a marketplace subsidised by the state. Australia also hasn't had the significant economic dislocation experienced by other countries in the past thirty years, which reduces the potency of people who ultimately feel like they are excluded and losing out to the opportunities of liberalisation and integration.[22]

This spirit of moderation is reflected in Matthew Lesh's *Democracy in a divided Australia*. He argues that while there is a contest for dominant values in Australia, the tension is not yet at a point of conflict. He prefers to highlight the divide between the 'Inners' and 'Outers'. In Lesh's words, "Inners pursue technocratic and paternalistic governance by the supposedly best and brightest, that is decision making by themselves. The growth and complexity of the regulatory state empowers Inners to make policy in their interests, often excluding Outers' voices".[23] Inners are "highly educated professional knowledge economy workers, the instinctive cultural progressives who reside in the inner city". Inners comprise an economic left "new elite": Highly educated Greens, Inner-city progressive Labor and the economic right that are "the old establishment" of the inner-city middle. By comparison, Outers "grew up and live in Outer surburbia, small towns and rural Australia . . . are unlikely to have gone to university, have low to middle incomes, are a bit older and more likely to be married and have kids" and "likely to be in jobs that require physical activity".[24] Outers are divided on the economic left between "the left behind" working-class Labor tradition and "the aspiration" Liberals. As Lesh astutely observes:

> There are few marginal seats made up of Inners. That is, contests between The New Elite[25] and The Left Behind,[26] between Labor and the Greens, are rare. Electoral battlelines between The Old Establishment[27] and The New Elite, between Labor, Liberals and Greens are even rarer.[28]

All four analyses point to a similar theme: the idea that there's a divide in society between those of us in well-paid outward looking jobs dependent on a good education and who are properly more tolerant and relativist; and those of us who struggle to make ends meet and are more vulnerable to forces outside their control, and who seek greater security. It'd be hard to argue with the global changes in the workplace—particularly in developed countries—where globalisation and freer trade shifted low-skill jobs offshore, while higher-skill jobs grew, leaving many behind. Internationalisation also brings with it more cosmopolitanism and greater tolerance. In Western liberal democracies, the neo-liberal era of equity extraction has concluded with some individuals enjoying the benefits of economic, cultural, and social liberalism that has prioritised their freedom. Then there are those that have been left behind because the equity that was extracted (however inefficiently) was often for their benefit and in many cases has been transferred to developing countries through jobs for competitive labour in return for cheaper goods. If the whole world were one country, this might be politically sustainable. But when people are divided into countries, it is clearly not sustainable. That necessitates a rethink about what is needed for those that have been left behind to be empowered and have the freedom to take responsibility for their own lives.

In short, there's a divide between concentrations of capital and a lack of access to capital: geographic proximity, the accumulation of wealth, and political and cultural influence. The consequence is that the political boundaries of society are being redrawn. In part, it comes down to whether people can harness these opportunities. It is clear that intentionally, or otherwise, the 2016 American presidential election redrew the boundaries of American society, leading to the election of Donald Trump. The same occurred with Brexit, when a single national constituency was given a voice and the traditional weighting given to established voices and institutions was drowned out by the weight of the whole of the population. The same might be said of the 2019 Australian federal election, which saw support for the Coalition in inner-urban seats taking electoral dives, while all seats won by the Coalition from Labor were located in the middle to outer suburbs. The absence of a single issue or figure in a nationwide election should, however, temper any enthusiasm that it was a direct translation of the theses discussed above.

Even so, each analysis's conclusion identifies a broader symptom of the divide. For liberalism to have an enduring constituency, it can't simply be a translation of philosophy into the language of a new vested interest that can secure 5% support from the voting public. To do so would mean continually changing principles and abandoning consistency. The enduring strength of liberalism is that it fundamentally speaks to the aspirations of all individuals and has the capacity to secure majority support because they can see their lives lived through the values it projects. Hence it is equally important to understand the building blocks that lead to individuals identifying with one vision for society or another.

The thought that there are 'Somewhere Outers' means that some individuals have been fundamentally left behind because the opportunities that used to exist are closed to them or were never available. That is partly true. It also reflects the structural imbalances between different sections of society. What actually matters, however, is identifying the causes that stop individuals living their best lives. That is a much bigger challenge than we recognise. It poses a great challenge to the viability of liberalism. For liberalism to address these gaps, liberals must take a step back, and reflect on why average people buy into liberal democracy in the first place. It is because liberal democracy enables individuals to live out their fullest lives.

5

Generation confrontation

Liberalism's demography

As we discussed in Chapter 1, the advancement of liberalism is really about the empowerment of individuals, but that also depends on equality of opportunity and an open society in which individuals are able to move throughout their lifecycle. The strength of liberalism is that it empowers individuals to live their fullest lives through their equal dignity, equality of opportunity, and the capacity to engage economically, socially, and culturally—constrained only by their own initiative and to do no harm to others. That is what makes it a uniting philosophy and a mode of government for everyone. That is liberalism's greatest strength—and weakness. It is its strength because it enables a mass constituency of people to see their lives and success realised through liberal values. It is its weakness because, in speaking to the full breadth of people's lives and choices, it does not corral individuals around a vested interest.

It is also what makes Australian liberalism so anodyne. As we outlined in Chapter 2, Australian liberalism is inherently non-ideological and focuses on how it practically reflects the sentiments and aspirations of individuals rolling through different stages of life. People's electoral support for liberalism reflects their lifecycle movements. There is no rote approach. How people vote can be informed by their values, their family's voting behaviour, learned ideology, simple lived experience, or the events they confront today. But there are adages that reflect the general sentiment of most people's lives, described in the numerous derivatives of the popular saying that "if you don't vote left under forty you have no heart, and if you don't vote right over forty you have no brains". There are different derivatives of this saying depending on the country—Labor v Liberal in Australia, Labour v Conservative in the United Kingdom, and Liberal v Conservative in the United States—but the spirit is the same. There are two parts to the logic of this oft trotted-out quip. The first is that, as people age, they simply learn more and that leads them to reject the progressive and possibly revolutionary spirit of a youthful worldview. And that is partly true. Maturity and learning can bring with them an understanding of the importance of institutions that you participate in or rely on. But the more important interpretation is that, as people move through life, their priorities change.

Australia's changing demographics

It's common to cite demography as destiny, particularly when we look at how birthrates and the ethnic origins of populations can reshape societies. The demography of age will reshape societies in forthcoming years and, with them, the constituency of liberalism.

The ageing population has become a staple of the public policy zeitgeist. Technology and access to better health services are improving our quality of life and life expectancy concurrently. And— no doubt surprising to many—the same generation is the primary beneficiary of the tax and transfer system through expenditure on the rising cost of pensions, aged care, healthcare, and the pharmaceutical benefits scheme. The analysis in a 2008 Productivity Commission report found that health expenditure for persons above the age of 65 are three times higher than for persons under 65. The same analysis found that the Pharmaceutical Benefits Scheme costs for Australians aged between 65 and 74 are twenty times higher than those for a person aged 15 to 24. And around 80% of costs were associated with managing conditions which technology has enabled them to shift from being terminal conditions to ones that can be chronically managed, and often a patient is being treated for multiple conditions concurrently.[1] This economic cost is felt in both the public funding model for health, as well as the private insurance. The cross-subsidisation is leading many young people to opt out of private health insurance. As a consequence there is a smaller group of people with higher needs pooling insurance, which means more people don't take it up and it becomes a self-reinforcing cycle of decline. And as new treatments and technology come along the options increase but the costs also rise because they're more specialised and needed longer.

The ageing population is not just a factor that affects Australia. In fact, we are less impacted. Most Western countries are experiencing some increase in the average age of their populations. They're outpaced by countries that have limited immigration (Japan) or that have constrained population growth (China). According to World

Population Prospects, countries like China and India will have median populations in the mid-40s and mid-50s respectively within thirty years. By comparison, high-immigration countries like Australia and the United States generally have a lower median population, although it is still ageing.

Table 1 | Median age of the population

Location	1980	2020	2030	2050
World	22.6	30.9	33.0	36.2
China	21.9	38.4	42.6	47.6
Japan	32.5	48.4	52.1	54.7
Australia	29.3	37.9	40.0	41.8
New Zealand	27.9	38.0	40.0	43.7
United Kingdom	34.4	40.5	42.4	44.5
Canada	29.2	41.1	43.0	45.5
United States	30.0	38.3	39.9	42.7

Source: World Population Prospects

There are considerable social and economic consequences that follow as a population ages. But the general proposition is that an ageing population disguises more unique shifts in the population profile of countries, including Australia, and that flows through to electoral behaviour.

Census data reveals the impact of the shifting age profile of the Australian population. A histogram of the population in 1901 resembles a pyramid with few older people, who could loosely be defined as above the age of 50. The cost of the Second World War is apparent when you assess the same data set in 1951, in which there is a significant reduction in the waistline of the graph, reflecting the loss of young adults, and particularly men, as well as the birth of the Baby Boomer generation. This generation's prominence is clear in the girth of middle-aged people in the 2001 census data, and in the improvement in lifespans, particularly for women. Until recently, the conclusion that most people have consistently drawn from the Baby Boomer bulge is that they are the largest and most influential generation. That is, until they weren't any longer the bulge.

Table 2 | Percentage of population in different age groups, actual and projected

As at June	0-17	18-35	36-64	65+
1980	30.5	29.9	29.9	9.6
1990	26.7	29.5	32.7	11.1
2000	24.9	26.0	36.7	12.4
2010	23.0	25.6	37.9	13.6
2020	22.5	25.0	36.4	16.1
2030	21.9	23.4	36.1	18.6
2040	20.9	23.4	35.8	20.0
2050	20.5	22.8	35.8	20.9

Source: World Population Prospects

By 2018, Australian Bureau of Statistics data showed that Millennials had staged "a dramatic demographic takeover".[2] They were now on course to become the most populous generation, providing a direct counterbalance to the traditional influence of Baby Boomers (with Generation X squeezed in the middle). According to Australian Bureau of Statistics data, in 2020, those aged between 18 and 35 are now 23.42% of the population, which is approaching the size of the age profile that is most likely to be economically productive—36 to 55.[3]

The shifting balance of generations in demography matters because it brings with it different attitudes and electoral behaviour based on the subgroups' life experiences. There is no single way to frame generational subgroups, but the commonly identified ones are:

- Builders, 1925–1945

- Baby Boomers, 1946–1964

- Generation X, 1965–1979

- Generation Y or Millennials, 1980–1994

- Generation Z, 1995–2009

- Generation Alpha, 2010–present[4]

Shaping a generation's worldview

The reality of generations isn't just the circumstances that they're born into and have lived through. It is always the current experience they share at specific stages of life that informs each generation's priorities. In people's late teens, their priorities will largely be around economic scarcity and their education—because that is what informs their decision-making at that moment. At the other end of the spectrum, retirees talk about their health, their grandkids, and economic security. Those different priorities sit at the heart of the dichotomy between the young and the old—opportunity versus security.

There is no single method of defining a generation, nor how they can easily be lumped together. Generalisations about generations can often seem to have as much credibility as a horoscope. But regardless of the inaccuracy of talking in this way, it is difficult to ignore the shared experiences that generations have—ranging from key world events to economic circumstances, cultural influences, and technology—and how these experiences shape their worldview. Every generation both inherits the compounding knowledge of those that have come before them and the shared experiences that have shaped society's outlook, as well as living shared experiences in their lifetime. It is hard to ignore the profound influence that the First and Second World Wars, as well as the Great Depression, can have on a generation's outlook. In my age bracket, we all had grandparents whose trademark was prudence because they'd 'lived through the war', or 'survived the Blitz', and 'learned it during the Depression'. For Generation X, their adulthood was shaped during an era of the end of the Cold War and the 1990s recession, the adoption of information technology and the internet, as well as September 11. Millennials shared many of these experiences, but were also the first generation to be digital native, to be conscience of climate change, and to have borne the brunt of Covid-19 pandemic and its economic legacy.

They're probably the most extreme examples, but the same cultural relevance occurs for those who remember a time before television, or computers, or—in my case—the internet and mobile phones. (I still remember what it was like to call someone to tell them where you'd meet and when, and the real inconvenience of being stood up, as well as how to use a telephone book or a road map, and the value of writing down a phone number!) These events shape who we are, what we prioritise, and how we see the world.

We often neglect the fact that most people approach politics based on the current stage of their life. When people are young, they have little and therefore nothing to lose, and seek out opportunity to build a life. As people progress through life, they accumulate wealth from the opportunities presented, and progressively shift to protect it as the basis of their security, particularly, as they become vulnerable in old age.

These challenges are exacerbated as modern technology extends the length and quality of people's lives. People may never have known how long they live, nor the length of their working life. What has changed is the timeframe that they're likely to live beyond in retirement. It was once assumed it would only be a few years, or around five percent of their life. Today, the length of retirement is trending toward a quarter of a person's adult life, and for many nearly a third. Critically, during that timeframe people are increasingly vulnerable and isolated. And if they run out of money, they can't just go back to work. It is a time in life when security is paramount. It inevitably raises issues of insecurity as people don't know the length of their life and what is necessary to conserve the quality of life they are used to for themselves and their spouse. The electoral consequences are real. As the demographer, Bernard Salt, observed, the reality of the generational divide is stirring but will dominate much of the debate in 2020:

> While it is true that boomers saw off this challenge at the May [2019] election, underlying age-based tensions remain. We see signs everywhere, including blatant ageism in advertising campaigns that portray boomers as universally enriched and technologically inept. And this summer's bushfires have been interpreted as the self-evident manifestation of climate-change denial—now very much perceived as a generational issue. Indeed, the rise of teenage activist Greta Thunberg has taken the issue of climate change and repositioned it as a matter of right versus wrong, of young versus old. Thunberg bypasses the millennials and speaks directly to boomers, whom she held accountable in her "how dare you" speech.[5]

The divide that reflects people's changing attitudes is the dichotomy between opportunity and security. Young people have a natural interest in opportunity because they have little investment in the status quo. Longevity is on their side, and they need an open society to drive their own success. Older people have a natural interest in security as they have accumulated interests. They are at a stage of life when you become more vulnerable over time and your interests are advanced by protecting what you have. It plays out in a relatively linear fashion across people's lifecycles.

When voters are youthful (up to their mid-20s), they're interested in educational and economic opportunities. In their mid-30s, people's focus shifts to career progress, repaying student debt, saving for a home, and forming a family. This is the opportunity stage of life. Younger people are on the journey to establishing themselves and have limited investment in the status quo, for example access to cheap housing and rent, and assistance in building themselves up. While liberalism offers them an open society of opportunity, conservatism offers them little, and socialism can possibly offer shortcuts until the tax bill needs to be paid.

From people's 30s to 50s, they're in their peak tax-paying period and accumulating wealth. As people turn to their mid-50s, they're generally setting their children free to the world, and become focused on their retirement and economic security. Depending on the decisions they make in or around this stage of life, their attitudes can shift from being focused on opportunity to converting to security, such as having a family with children to protect, a career or business whose success can determine their income, and assets that can define their capacity for financial security and leverage.

It is also an error to lump all older people in together. For instance, in 2020, the combined population over 56 is 25.42% of the total population. Those over 66 are only 15% of the population. Telling people under 60 they're old isn't likely to go down well. But it is also a misdiagnosis of their attitude to life. People in their 50s and early 60s, and increasingly late 60s, are likely to still be working, paying tax, viewing retirement as a distant prospect, and, although experiencing age-related health complications, are unlikely to be substantially limited in their life choices. People in their late 60s and early 70s are likely to be comfortable in retirement, with children off their hands and enjoying the fruits of their working life. That experience then shifts as people enter their late 70s and 80s, as they begin to experience restrictions on their lifestyles because of ill health and a tendency towards economic risk aversion.

Of course, this analysis is not a perfect reflection of every individual's life. Someone can spend their whole life being a committed socialist as they own their own home, and likewise someone could be a committed conservative in their early 20s. But the alignment of interest is clear.

Older and younger voters

Societies have never had as many older people as they have now. That is a statement of the obvious, yet it has significant implications. It has led to a series of policy measures in Australia based on recommendations in intergenerational reports that assess the long-term budgetary consequences for governments. Former Treasurer, Peter Costello, was the first to commission such a report. It has been periodically updated to inform public policy discussion. Costello's report raised questions about how a society can fund itself as the number of people not working increases, and the share of those who are working decreases. The report also raises questions about tax rates. In particular, what tax burden ought people owe at different stages of their life, and is there a point at which they should 'max-out' their contributions? How does a society fund services for a generation in retirement who require public health, pensions, pharmaceuticals, and aged care at an ever increasing cost to public expenditure?

What such analysis often fails to notice is that societies have never had so many younger people, while concurrently having so many older people as well. This has the effect of narrowing the 'in-between'.

The generational risk presented to Australian society is the extent to which generational interests reflect the priorities of government. No comprehensive study has been completed in Australia, however, the Pew Research Center has completed analysis assessing the attitudinal shifts of younger and older people toward budget tradeoffs in the United States. Perhaps surprisingly, younger people are more fiscally prudent, with 41% of those aged between 18 and 29 believing that reducing the deficit is a higher priority than preserving social security and Medicare. But 66% of those aged 65 and older support preserving social security and Medicare, compared to 21% of who support reducing the deficit. The same generational attitudes also reflect where people think government resources should be focused with 50% of those aged 18-29 believing public spending should be focused on younger adults, compared to 34% on older adults. Of those aged over 65, only 15% support a focus on younger adults, whereas 48% support a focus on older adults.[6]

The divergence in attitudes is hardly surprising. Research completed in 2008 found that when "asked to rate their present life on a scale of zero to 10, [Baby] Boomers, on average, give their lives a rating of 6.2, [compared to] adults younger than boomers (those who are ages 18 to 41) give their lives an average rating of 6.5".[7]

The attitudinal divide was highlighted in international research looking at the importance of national identity. While Australians generally do not believe that birthplace is important to national identity, 19% of those over the age of 50 think it is important, compared with

4% of those aged 18-34.[8] The division is more pronounced when it comes to the importance attached to national customs and traditions, which 40% of 18-34-year-olds think are important, compared with 60% of those over 50.

This is not a specifically Australian trend. A study into age and generational effects on turnout in Australian federal elections found "the decline in turnout in democracies around the world amongst young people is not simply an age issue, but is a generational issue . . . recently generations are less likely to vote across their entire life . . . [and] any tendency for younger generations to not vote would need to be counterbalanced by growing turnout in older generations".[9] But the future does not belong to older generations.

The practical electoral consequences are stark. Australian Electoral Commission data shows that first time voters have a high electoral turnout at around 94%, before declining below to around 90% and progressively recovering at a relatively static rate of 95% between 40 and 65, before declining again.[10] High engagement at a first federal election can be attributed to "peer engagement".

Recent elections in the United Kingdom have demonstrated this trend starkly. The divide between voting behaviour led YouGov analysts to conclude "age seems to be the new dividing line in British politics",[11] and "class would tell you little more about a person's voting intention than looking at their horoscope or reading their palms . . . in electoral terms, age is the new class".[12]

Clearly, Brexit was one of the most defining issues of our time, and younger—more globally orientated—Britons voted to remain. Aspects of that legacy continued through the two subsequent British general elections. But it would be a misdiagnosis of the whole motivation, particularly because so much of Jeremy Corbyn's agenda as leader of the Labour Party in 2017 and 2019 focused on wealth redistribution and provided a limited solution for the United Kingdom's Brexit dilemma. Electoral data from 2017 shows that for first-time voters aged 18-19, the gap between the Tories and Labour was 47%, with only 66% voting Labour to 19% for the Tories. These numbers were reversed for those over 70, with 69% voting Tory and 19% voting Labour. Only people in the age bracket over 60 showed a majority were voting Tory. Despite the relatively binary nature of the 2019 election, the numbers didn't change radically with only a couple of points difference—with people aged over 70 voting Tory by a margin of 67% to 14% Labour. This led analysts to conclude that "for every 10 years older a person is, the likelihood they voted Conservative increases by 9 points".[13]

In part, it can be explained by a Social Market Foundation poll in 2017 that found Corbyn's Labour had double the support of sub-45 voters, who think Labour is "on their side", unlike the Conservatives.[14] At the time, the Foundation's director was quoted as saying:

> The Conservatives' problem is that you can't expect people to support an economic settlement in which they have literally no stake. But years of stagnant wages and a dysfunctional housing market mean that many people are reaching their late 30s and 20s having worked hard for years, but are still unable to amass significant savings and or make a decent contribution to a pension, or buy a home.[15]

Similar trends can be found in the United States. In the 2016 American presidential election, voters under the age of 40 were far more likely to support Hillary Clinton, compared to people over the age of 40, who supported Donald Trump. The critical difference is that while the group that voted most strongly for Clinton—18 to 24-year-olds—only represented 10% of the vote, the two age groups—50 to 64 and 65 and older—that voted most strongly for Trump amounted to 45% of the total vote.[16]

The attitudes of young Australians could be dismissed as simply a reflection of young people always thinking politicians are out of touch. But it raises questions about their confidence in our democracy. As outlined in Chapter 3, there has been a dramatic decline in public trust and faith in some of our most important institutions, including our democracy. The correlation between the seeming inertia of institutions and public confidence is real. This was practically experienced in the difference between voting behaviour in 2017 for the postal survey on marriage for same-sex couples, and the 2019 federal election. The postal survey led to enrolment rates amongst young Australians that resulted in the 2019 electoral roll being the most complete in Australian history.[17] Yet, within 18 months, turnout for the 2019 federal election saw a collapse in young voter participation.[18] In the lead up to the same-sex marriage postal survey, 65,274 young Australians jumped on the roll and participated.[19] Yet by the 2019 federal election, there was the lowest turnout in an election (less than 91%) since compulsory voting was introduced.[20] And the turnout was lowest in electorates with the highest share of younger voters. The explanation could be simply that the survey concerned an issue they cared about. But there might be another explanation. If they responded to the postal survey, there was a direct link to an outcome. The same doesn't quite occur in a general election. There's a direct connection to someone who gets elected. But that's an indirect connection to a government being elected, or a policy being implemented. The proximity between action and outcome is loose, whereas in the case of the postal survey it was tight.

The reason for such a stark turnaround is not clear. But the two polls highlight the significance of the relationship between casting a vote and a concrete outcome. The postal survey had an explicit link to electoral behaviour and a change in the law on an issue that enjoyed the overwhelming support of younger people, and ultimately most Australians. Federal elections involve a package of issues. Many of the electorates that have large younger populations—notably in capital cities—rarely decide elections. So the policies that matter to younger voters are rarely implemented.

The consequences are not just electoral, but economic, when the population consists of significant numbers of older and younger people. As an Oxford Economics study found:

> The intergenerational redistributional tension is intrinsic in life cycle models. Young cohorts have few assets and wages are the main source of income. Old generations work less and prefer a high rate of return from their savings. When the government has access to lump-sum taxes and transfers, redistributive policy need not resort to distortionary measures (such as capital taxes or inflation).[21]

The consequence is a progressive conversion in attitude and sentiment. Those who have nothing to lose are far more attracted to political ideals of redistribution and idealism. They seek economic and educational opportunity for themselves and are allured by socialism's false promises. As people progress through life events, their attitude shifts from idealism to securing what they have earned. Unsurprisingly, those who don't secure assets have little to conserve. Private property and homeownership remain central to any attitudinal shift. This matters for two reasons: first, the changing age profile of the Australian community and comparable nations; and, second, because of how people move through political attitudes as they move through lifecycle events. And this tension directly effects the constituency for liberalism.

6

Marrying your mortgage

How voters vote

Demographic trends play a critical role in the structure of society. This book is published in 2020. Just as we can't predict how technology will change, no one really knows where the world will be in 2050. The optimistic scenario is that the compounding influence of technology will lead us to a better world where individuals live longer, healthier, and happier lives. But that creates its own challenges. Longer lives inevitably lead us to consume more. Yet increases in consumption can be offset through efficiency improvements. The world's resources do not sit on a binary spectrum between finite and infinite. But it does pose challenges for employment from automation and the extent economies can survive through service provision (particularly when tested with pandemics), and limitations still constrain access to some resources, such as land.

As outlined in Chapter 2, Australian liberalism is unique, when compared with dominant forms of liberalism embraced in other countries, in its commitment to conserving the cultural and institutional status quo. This commitment is tempered by its other commitment, namely the need for a sense of liberal justice to maintain liberalism's social license. It's that social license that informs the breadth of liberalism's constituency. Alas, rather than expanding, liberalism's social license is currently heading in the wrong direction.

As explained in the previous chapter, liberalism's diminishing acceptance by the electorate can be seen across the Western world. At elections, increasing numbers of the largest age demographic groups are supporting candidates who espouse socialism such as Jeremy Corbyn in Britain and Bernie Sanders in America. While that trend has always existed, its strength is increasing significantly.

Evidence can be found in the Australian National University's Australian Electoral Study. Whilst the divide in the most recent Australian federal election was not as pronounced as that witnessed in recent British and American elections, it does demonstrate that age is a key determinant in how voters connect with competing views of the nation. This leads ANU to conclude that:

> While young voters are moving further to the left, older voters are moving to the right. Among those 55 and over, 18% more voted Liberal than Labor in the 2019 election, which is the greatest Liberal lead among this age group since the AES began in 1987. Overall the evidence from the Australian Election Study is consistent with a growing generational divide in the voting behavior of younger and older Australians.

It is concerning that this trend is becoming more pronounced over time. At the 2004 election, nearly 50% of Australians under the age of 35 were voting Liberal, and today it is now down to 23%. At the same time, while support for the Labor Party has also declined, support for the Greens has increased, meaning that they now secure more than 28% of the vote.

There is, of course, no perfect overlap between voting behaviour and a commitment to liberalism. You can be motivated by several liberal commitments and vote for different parties. Depending on your understanding of the Greens' political values, you might see their increasing appeal to the electorate either as a positive or negative development for liberalism. The Greens have a mixed political tradition of old school socialism and environmentalism, as well as a liberal social outlook and views on internationalism and some economic matters that might be regarded as being liberal. But when 89% of Greens voters report that climate change is "extremely important" to them and 68% identify the environment as their "most important" election issue, it is difficult to say that the philosophy of liberalism is the key motivator in their electoral behavior.

What's apparent is that Australia's demographic profile is moving away from liberal democracy anchored in individual empowerment through responsibility, and toward social democracy focused on collective empowerment. This is not a trend that is just identified amongst younger voters. The same study found that on a 'left' versus 'right' scale, where 0 is far-left and 10 is far-right with a midpoint of 5, the average Australian identifies as centre-right at 5.46 in 1996, whereas at more recent elections the average Australian has moved to 4.91 and 4.98.[1] Of course, such a spectrum gives little clarity about how people interpret 'left' and 'right', and whether they can be easily transposed for 'socialist' or 'liberal'. Many voters have strong opinions on free markets, but privately have little concern or engagement on cultural or social policy. Yet arguably many of the latter debates have become the organizing issues for parties of the centre-right after the major liberal economic reforms implemented from the 1980s through to the early 2000s.

Younger voters' attitudes

The shifting attitudes of younger Australians matter because of their demographic takeover and because of the extreme shifts that are occurring internationally. Globally, millennials overtook baby boomers in the mid-1990s and "based on sheer numbers alone, the 'millennial moment' is more a story of developing countries and global progress than the advertising stereotypes of affluent urban youth prevalent in the western media and marketing".[2]

A study by the Australian Futures Project looked at the perfect candidate for the twenty-first century. These studies are often unreliable because, when asked a theoretical question, people respond to their political aspirations for candidates, and this is not always the same as what drives their voting behaviour. The study found the somewhat predictable conclusion that Millennials and Generation Z are focused on keeping the cost of living down, climate, health, education, and honest government. But what might surprise people is that the older generation didn't much care about keeping down taxes.[3] The divergence of intergenerational tension cannot be understated. While it only lived a short run, the ABC's *Tonightly with Tom Ballard* was full of segments where Gen Ys beat up on their Boomer parents. In one episiode, the removal of some tax concessions would lead to Boomers only be able to take one first-class overseas trip each year, and the sale of one of many investment properties to make ends meet. A column in *The Age* started with the opening sentences, "Here's some breaking news for Baby Boomers. You've had a very good run and you're just about done".[4] Similarly, the Grattan Institute's analysts claimed in 2017, following the UK election that stripped Theresa May of her majority and nearly installed Corbyn as Prime Minister, that "the young are coming".[5]

The critical issue for liberals is to identify the core drivers of this political behaviour, which lead to younger people no longer identifying with the ambitions of a liberal order, and preferring those of a socialist alternative. It is a topic discussed extensively in literature assessing generational attitudes in Western liberal democracies.

Challenges faced by young people

In *The Pinch: How the Baby Boomers took their children's future—and why they should give it back*, former British Conservative MP, David Willetts identifies the divide that ultimately explains the electoral behaviour. It is driven, he maintains, by the different economic experiences of younger and older generations. Willetts concludes that "our fears about our society and the strains in our economy reflect a breakdown in the balance between the generations", and reflect the shift in political sentiment that has led to a more radical-left younger polity.[6] He argues that there is no revolution against bourgeois values. People still aspire to have a good job, family, and home but "we are finding it harder to achieve them".[7] Put simply younger generations (and younger individuals) are finding it harder to realise very basic life ambitions for job, family, and home through what is perceived as a liberal economic order, and increasingly look for radical alternatives that appear to offer them a pathway.

Similar themes have emerged in the United States, with a columnist for *The Atlantic*, Anne Lowrey, identifying the risks of "the great affordability crisis"[8] that is breaking the country. While Lowrey identifies a series of metrics that highlights the gap in affordability, some of which are unique to the American system, such as healthcare, it is the affordability of housing that is structurally changing people's lives as individuals and families:

> One central effect of the housing-cost crisis has been to turn the United States into a country of renters. The homeownership rate has fallen from a peak of nearly 70 percent in the mid-aughts to under 65 percent today; the numbers are more acute for Millennials, whose homeownership rate is 8 percentage points lower than that of their parents at the same age. Unable to buy, roughly 3.5 million younger families have kept renting—delaying the Millennial and Gen X cohorts' wealth accumulation, thus consigning them to worse net-worth trajectories for the rest of their lives. And renting, for many families, is not affordable, either: Nearly half of renters are facing uncomfortable monthly bills, and the cost of renting has risen faster than renters' incomes for a full 20 years now.[9]

The problem of affordability in the United States affects tertiary education almost as much as healthcare, as a result of different systems for paying fees. The perceived intergenerational impact of climate change—those alive today will only be marginally impacted, compared with future generations, who will experience profound changes—also brings it into the intergenerational dialogue, as well as traditional environmental and economic policy. The consequences experienced in the United States, the United Kingdom, and Australia have hollowed the political constituency for the liberal status quo. This is demonstrated in the focus of political candidates.

In his political manifesto leading up to the 2019 British election, Jeremy Corbyn, made a series of commitments that reflected generational concerns under the banner of "It's time for real change". Housing was core, including a commitment to a "new social housebuilding programme of more than a million homes over a decade, with council housing at its heart. By the end of the Parliament we will be building at an annual rate of at least 150,000 council and social homes, with 100,000 of these built by councils for social rent in the biggest council housebuilding programme in more than a generation".[10] In education, the pitch was more explicit—"abolish tuition fees".[11] The areas of disagreement between the Conservatives and the Labour about climate change had narrowed, with both committed to similar targets. This meant that the intergenerational components of climate change in "The Future is Ours" Youth Manifesto focused on industrial and skills development.[12]

Climate change has remained a divisive electoral issue in the United States. A core promise of Sanders's electoral platform was a "Green New deal" to promote "10 percent renewable energy" and "a just transition for communities and workers". This was one of a number of priorities, including the uniquely American need for "Medicare for all" though a "single-payer, national health insurance program".[13] Sanders also promised "College for all", which would involve cancelling "all student loan debt for the some 45 million Americans who owe about $1.6 trillion", as well as "Housing for all" by "ending the housing crisis by investing $2.5 trillion to build nearly 10 million permanently affordable housing units" and making "rent affordable".[14]

The young feel disenfranchised

It's hardly surprising that these electoral promises are attractive to a generation that feel disenfranchised from the established liberal economic order. This is a generation, after all, that perceives themselves to be burdened by compounding economic and environmental debt, while older generations seem to be relieved of any burden. This presents a serious challenge for liberalism. The challenge is not to address an event that temporarily changes the circumstances of younger generations. There is no reason to believe that these people's voting behaviour will change as they grow older. Rather, we need to accept that this generation's experiences have brought about a profound change in their attitudes, and a conviction that governance, society, and economics are all in sharp decline in meeting their needs.

In the United States, the libertarian *Reason Foundation* completed a study in 2014 assessing the sentiments and attitudes of Millennials. It investigated their likely electoral impact and the counter-cultural values they seemed to espouse as a generation. It observed that this is the first generation to be digital natives and grow up in a globalized world. In the American context, Millennials also prove interesting because they were part of an electoral "surge" and had "shifted markedly left in their voting behavior over the past decade".[15] The study is of critical significance because it investigated what led this change in behaviour.

The survey assessed the basis upon which Millennials identified as 'independent'. It concluded that "they are social liberals and fiscal centrists with the potential to become more fiscally conservative as they age".[16] People's political views change as their lived experience reshapes their priorities and worldview. The survey found that the core driver for people to go on a journey of conversion from identifying as politically 'independent' to Republican occurred around when they got married and/or bought a home. The process of getting married and owning a home themselves are is not the sole determinant of a person's voting behaviour, but this data is indicative.

Little platoons to little capitalists

Marriage and home ownership necessarily share much in common and often occur around the same time in life. Marriage—especially when combined with parenthood—acts as a similar form of investment in the existing social order and becomes a point of self-motivated interest in security and stability. Of course the ideal of marriage as the foundation for family has changed significantly in the past fifty years. Traditionally, marriage was a concept that was the primary formal expression of consensual, mutually dependent relationships beyond those we secure through birth. Today it can take broader forms through marriage-like relationships, such as de facto relationships. The societal shift has been from a rigid idea of 'family values' toward the looser idea of 'valuing families', but the fundamental obligations and responsibilities don't change.

What makes ownership and marriage more politically relevant is they are both investments in the status quo and provide the foundation for family as an expression of the strength of two individuals. Owning your home invariably also involves a significant sunk investment and being hostage to a mortgage. Individuals who own homes have an investment in the existing economic order and are wedded to the interests of economic progress. Home ownership also acts as a form of economic, social, and family security against other forms of instability.

In his *Reflections on the Revolution in France*, Edmund Burke, extolled the virtues of 'little platoons' as the foundation for society reflecting people's shared interest in being held in the good standing of others with whom we share social solidarity:

One of the first symptoms they reveal of a selfish and mischievous ambition is a profligate disregard of the dignity they share with others… to love the little platoon we belong to in society is the first principle (the germ as it were) of public affections. It is the first link in the chain by which we proceed towards a love to our country and to mankind. The interests of that portion of social arrangement (the 'little platoon' we belong to) is a trust in the hands of all those who compose it; and as none but bad men would justify it in abuse, none but traitors would barter it away for their own personal advantage.[17]

Of course, the smallest of little platoons are individuals that form families. Families are the ultimate expression of voluntary mutual dependency between individuals, and the most intimate forms of trusts. It is only with the foundation of such trusts and the security they can afford that individuals carry the first true weight of responsibility beyond themselves, and the shared interest for their advancement to the benefit of others. Yet the economic relationship between private property and family is also critical, as Burke observes:

The power of perpetuating our property in our families is one of the most valuable and interesting circumstances belonging to it, and that which tends the most to the perpetuation of society itself. It makes our weakness subservient to our virtue, it grafts benevolence even upon avarice.[18]

In his analysis of *The Russian Revolution*, the respected historian, Richard Pipes, observes the critical socio-political role of private property in entrenching the status quo:

Private property is arguably the single most important institution of social and political integration. Ownership of property creates a commitment to the political and legal order since the latter guarantees property rights: it makes the citizen into a co-sovereign, as it were. As such, property is the principal vehicle for inculcating in the mass of the population respect for law and an interest in the preservation of the status quo. Historical evidence indicates that societies with a wide distribution of property, notably in land and residential housing, are more conservative and stabler, and for that reason more resilient to upheavals of all sorts. Thus the French peasant, who in the eighteenth century was a source of instability became in the nineteenth, as a result of the gains of the French Revolution, a pillar of conservatism.[19]

In short, if you have don't have anything to conserve then you have nothing to lose. It's a seminal reason why individuals who are getting ahead will defend the status quo. These impacts are compounded even further when individuals have a mortgage and have a direct and explicit interest in securing the value of their property outright. For liberals property is the foundation for dignity and the reward for effort. But the value for liberals from property is much greater than a tradable title. Home ownership provides individuals, and often by extension families, the foundations to flourish. Psychologist, Abraham Maslow, outlined in his 1943 paper the importance of a hierarchy of needs to empower people to self-actualisation and achieve their full potential. The hierarchy represented as a pyramid has a broad foundation from basic needs to achieve psychological needs to achieve self-actualisation at its apex. Food, water and shelter provide the foundation for everything else. Without either a home to own or rent and provide shelter the very foundations of a life cannot be built. Similarly, it provides an environment that individuals can form families in security as a form of mutual dependency with a spouse, and intergenerational security with children to parents coupled with the environment that fosters values outside of the competing public square, and is the foundation of the strength of the nation.

In his *Forgotten People* speech Menzies articulated the liberal ideal of property and homes as a reflection of the "middle class" and a "a stake in the country", and expounded their value. He articulated homes in three modes "homes material, homes human, homes spiritual". His concept of homes material was "the concrete expression of the habits of frugality and saving ... to which we can withdraw, in which we may be among our friends, into which no stranger may come against our will" and that patriotism "inevitably springs from the instinct to defend and preserve our homes". Homes human is the centre of family and, in his case, "where my wife and children are" with "the instinct to give them a chance in life" through the transfer of values to instill the dignity of individual responsibility, work and education to "qualify" the next generation for society, and homes spiritual is the "independence of man" to stand on their own two feet as it is a "brave acceptance of unclouded individual responsibility".[20]

The contribution of homes and property is not just romantic or idealistic. Its economic contribution to enterprise with initiative and responsibility is essential. The leverage of capital that can only be realised through private property rights has an impact that far transcends its isolated economic value. Peruvian economist, Hernando de Soto, explains in *The Mystery of Capital* the connection between the economic power of private property and the success of capitalist societies. De Soto critically assesses the weaknesses of countries that failed to develop economically. He finds a common thread in each case, namely the absence of enforceable property rights. There is a disconnect between such countries and the opportunities afforded by the global economy for them. He explains that "only the Western nations and small enclaves of wealthy people in developing former communist nations have the capacity to represent assets and potential, and therefore, the ability to produce and use capital efficiently".[21] This capacity is required in order for domestic economies to grow, and to connect them into the potential of a globalised marketplace. Private property rights are essentially tied to a liberal conception of decentralised prosperity. If individuals cannot apply their labour and skill toward a tradable asset whose capital they can then risk for investment to secure future reward then we undermined their capacity to advance their self-empowerment. An open economy with private property provides the incentive for individual enterprise to pursue the creation of wealth to improve the available capital in the whole economy to support others and invest in the future.

This is a point that was well understood by Menzies and it has a critical role at the heart of Australian liberalism. In the speech in which he claimed victory in the 1949 election, Menzies identified home ownership as the foundation for 'little capitalists', not just because it creates the economic opportunity for investment, but also because the equity can be leveraged for other economic activity.[22] Many small businesses are founded with the security of a home to leverage for finance. Aside from their home, few people have the equity to move beyond an employee's salary.

With mutually supportive relationships (that we traditionally ascribe to marriages), home ownership entrenches liberal ideals because of the security consistent with the considerations of Maslow as the foundations for individuals to live their best lives, through the creation of an environment that fosters independence, responsibility, trust, mutual dependency and leverage for economic activity. And it clearly informs electoral behaviour too.

7

Disposable income avocados

Millennials' lifestyle

As outlined in Chapter 2, one of the foundational principles of the Crown colonies, and subsequently of modern Australia, was the relatively democratic distribution of land as a direct rejection of the European system of hereditary privilege and transfer of wealth amongst the few. This democratic ownership of land is a cornerstone for the thriving of liberalism in the Australian political tradition—it has created a liberal political class. Yet, when land ownership is concentrated, and even more so when homeownership is concentrated, we are seeing the reverse trend toward generations no longer seeing their life ambitions realised through liberal values.

In 2016, the demographer, Bernard Salt, wrote of the economic challenges facing Millennials. His article in *The Australian* begins: "If you are under 40 and starting to read this, I politely suggest that you turn the page".[1] It is his warning about the "truth bombs" that follow. Essentially, his argument is that the "Middle Aged Moralisers" were tired of Millennial complaints about the world that they are inheriting and the challenges they face, particularly around homeownership. But the biggest truth bomb, Salt writes, is brown on the outside, and green on the inside:

> I have seen young people order smashed avocado with crumbled feta on five-grain toasted bread at $22 a pop and more. I can afford to eat this for lunch because I am middle-aged and have raised my family. But how can young people afford to eat like this? Shouldn't they be economising by eating at home? How often are they eating out? Twenty-two dollars several times a week could go towards a deposit on a house.[2]

And there began the smashed avocado critique of Millennials complaining about housing affordability. As he acknowledged in a column a year later, it started a wildfire of condemnation including tweets that "I stopped eating smashed avocado . . . and now I own a castle".[3] The response was ridicule from the targets, but also found its home with those who managed to get ahead.

Similarly, in a 2017 interview on Channel Nine's Sixty Minutes program, a property developer, Tim Gurner, dismissed the concerns of younger Australians about saving to buy their own home. He identified conspicuous consumption as the root cause of their problem. Famously, he said, "When I was trying to buy my first home, I wasn't buying smashed avocado for $19 and four coffees at $4 each . . . we're at a point now where the expectations of younger people are very, very high."[4] The inflammatory nature of his commentary meant it went viral and avocados (especially when smashed on toast) have become emblematic of Millennials' economic challenges, apparent indulgences, and incapacity to buy a home.

It's certainly a popular comment from Baby Boomers on the quality of life enjoyed by their kids and grandkids. But it isn't just about avocados. Young people are awash with technology earlier generations lacked, and there is an appetite to have the latest. Younger people also have a much greater appetite for service economy 'experiences'— particularly international travel—and indulge this appetite in a way that earlier generations either could not or did not at any stage of life. At least for some Australians, the once-in-a-lifetime holiday to Europe or the United States is well and truly over. Data from 2016 shows that half the population has already travelled internationally by the age of forty, and only 12.9% now must wait until retirement.[5]

This trend has radically changed in my lifetime. When I was in secondary school, I remember the introduction of 'affordable' laptop computers in the expectation they would improve learning outcomes.[6] I also remember when the first 'history tour' was established for students with sufficient means to travel to Europe and visit the battlefields of the First World War. These had since become commonplace in independent schools until the Covid-19 outbreak that grounded the world's tourism sector. Similarly, international tertiary study was uncommon at universities, and is now built into many academic courses, aided by the opportunity of Fee-Help for travel and accommodation expenses.

This seeming generosity can only help reinforce the thought that young Australians have never had it so good, and if they just scaled it back, everything would be fine. This comes out in the data. Only 24% of people between the age of 18 and 34 believe housing is affordable, compared with 69% who say it is unaffordable; whereas 48% of people over 55 believe it is affordable, compared with 45% who say it is unaffordable.[7]

Increased cost of housing

What such analysis ignores is the fact that the fundamental problems preventing people from being able to afford to buy a home also plague the rental market. Data from the Australian Bureau of Statistics shows that rents have grown by 1,059% between 1972 and 2019, compared to an overall Consumer Price Index increase of 947% in the same timeframe.[8] That shouldn't really surprise. The impact on younger people is more extreme because they are more likely to move closer to capital cities in their early adulthood to access tertiary institutions and employment. The cost of quality rental accommodation around capital cities, where employment opportunities exist, face crunch points.

The higher the costs of rent, and the more it squeezes disposable incomes, the more difficult it is for individuals to save. It is one of the reasons that marriages or marriage-like relationships are greater than the sum of their parts. They are the most powerful social welfare system because they succeed through mutual dependency. But equally important is the fact that they promote the sharing of resources toward a common purpose. Put simply, couples can save faster than most individuals through pooling of their resources, and having a spouse to share the journey with likely encourages greater discipline too!

Australian Bureau of Statistics data shows that, over time, what is rising for all age groups is the demands on their income for essential costs, with the largest share taken for housing. Everyone has experienced at least some increase, and particularly those in the traditional first homeowner catchment around the mid-20s through to the mid-40s.[9] By comparison, there has been a general decline in the non-essential categories for younger Australians, while it has increased overall for Australians over 55.

Prices that rise as a result of consumer and market behaviour are one thing, but when it comes to public policy, governments shouldn't be compounding the problem faced by the young. The discussion of rising costs associated with an ageing population is not new. They have long been identified in Intergenerational Reports, particularly in relation to expectations of access to healthcare services and the Pharmaceutical Benefit Scheme at the stage of life when they are in the highest demand, and in which people depend upon pensions and aged care support. What is rarely compared is how that marries up with who is paying the revenue to support it.

Consequences of rising house prices

The consequences are clear. In 2015, the Productivity Commission completed a report into the tax and transfer incidence in Australia. The report assessed the consequences of the tax system on different sections of the community based on income and wealth. It also assessed the impact on people at different stages of life, and identified disturbing challenges confronting the nation.[10] The report found:

> The clearest age-related effect of the tax and transfer system is to redistribute income from families of working age to families of retirement age. Average net tax flows—taxes paid less transfers received—are positive across all age groups except for those aged 60+.

On average, families in the under-60 age groups pay $15,300 more per year in taxes than they receive in transfers. By contrast, families in the 60+ age group receive an average of $10,900 more in transfers than they pay in taxes. Families in the 60+ age group also pay the least in gross taxes and receive the most in gross transfers, largely because this age group is least likely to be working. In total, families in the 60+ age group account for 51 per cent of all transfer expenditure.[11]

And the basis for such a transfer is partly dominated by expenditure associated with ageing, but it is also because the predominant models of tax paid by individuals are income tax and the goods and services tax. Once people enter the pension phase of their superannuation, the overwhelming majority of Australians' income tax falls to zero even if they are still paying company tax through their investments, and in many cases that tax is refunded through dividend imputation.[12] And with some Australians over 60 still working, they continue to pay income tax, although many use flexibilities in the tax system to reduce their tax by transitioning to retirement or boosting their superannuation savings at a concessional tax rate. The practical reality for most Australians, once they reach retirement, is that they shift from actively earning income exposed to the highest tax rates, to passively earning retirement income with no tax rate, with their primary tax contribution made through the lowest tax rate: the 10% GST. With the Productivity Commission finding "average net taxes increase with age, peaking in middle age before declining as retirement approaches", because the share of the type of taxes paid as people age shifts away from income tax with marginal rates peaking in the mid-40% of income earned and toward consumption taxes at 10% of expenditure. And that assumes the GST is universally applied, when housing, fresh food, and medical products and services, which make up a high share of household expenditure, are GST free.[13]

Intergenerational justice

This does not gel with a liberal understanding of intergenerational justice. Our interdependence and a sense of social equity resolutely justifies older Australians being supported. At the same time, there is a lack of intergenerational justice when those who have had the opportunity to hold (and do hold) the wealth of a nation are paying lower tax rates while having the most redistributed to them by the taxpayer. This shifts the burden onto those who are striving to get ahead, who hold less wealth, and consume the least from the tax and transfer system. This occurs not just because of the tax and transfer system, but also because of the structure of how Australians accumulate and hold wealth. In most cases, individuals accumulate wealth through ownership of a home, other property, and superannuation; all of which attract some form of tax concession in accumulation, holding, income streams, or capital gains.

In practice, this amounts to a direct transfer from those who are 'having a go' to those who have 'had their go'. And it is only likely to get worse. Projections calculate that in 1989 a 40-year-old contributed approximately $3,000 per annum to support a Baby Boomer; that this contribution has since risen to around $7,000, and it is now projected to hit $12,000 by 2041.[14]

The economist, Judith Sloan, has explained that "Intergenerational injustice is a myth . . . The social compact runs along these lines: parents and often grandparents are involved in the rearing of children; parents are expected to work to provide for their children and their parents; one way or another, older folk who can no longer work are looked after".[15] Except that is only partly right.

In *The Pinch*, Willetts explains that, while younger generations have often supported their elders, it hasn't been on a trajectory of continuing improved standards of living. Willetts argues that, in British society:

> by and large the system takes money from middle-aged people and redistributes it to children and older people, not just through benefits but also in education and healthcare. This is rather like the redistribution that has traditionally been undertaken by the family and which to an extent still is. But as the family has shrunk so the welfare state has found itself doing more. And the welfare state tends to focus principally on the older generation, to which we do of course have inescapable obligations, whereas historically the flow of resources in families from both parents and grandparents has been to the younger generations.[16]

This has serious implications for liberalism. The flow from wealth transfers shifts the financial burden from earlier generations who have consolidated their wealth, onto later generations who are still improving their standard of living.

Demographics of homeownership

Of chief concern should be the continued rise in house prices. In the past thirty years, the price of housing as a ratio of a person's income has doubled, from 4.7 times annual household income to nine times.[17] The practical consequence has been homeownership in free fall as young people increasingly find it difficult to get their foot on the property ladder. It isn't just young people. The Australian Housing and Urban Research Institute analysed the thirty-year trend in home ownership in Australia by age group. Between 1986 and 2016, homeownership rates fell markedly. Only one age group saw an increase in long-term home ownership rates—those aged

65 to 74 years, which increased by only 0.1% (81.9% to 82%).[18] By comparison, 55-64 year-olds experienced a decline of 3.3% (81.3 to 78%), 45-44 year-olds 6.8% (81.3 to 71.7%), those aged 35-44 years and 25-34 years both dropping 11% (off 73.2 to 62.2% for 35-44 year-olds and 55.6 to 44.6%) and a more modest reduction of 15-24 year-olds by 1% off a low base (24% to 23.1%).[19] And the trend is clear when comparing the average age of a purchaser and owner. In 1998, purchasers and owners were respectively 38 and 58 years-old, demonstrating that it took twenty years for Australians to pay off their 'Castle'. In 2015, the respective ages were 45 and 67 years-old, leading to a seven-year increase in the age of the average purchaser and a nine-year increase in the age of an owner, extending the repayment timeframe to twenty-two years.[20]

Household, Income and Labour Dynamics in Australia (HILDA) survey data shows a similar trend. Homeownership rates were always going to be low amongst young Australians under the age of 24, but even then, it has more than halved between 2002 and 2014 from 6.2% to only 2.4%. But the largest drop as a share is 12.6% for Australians between 35 and 39 from 61% in 2002 to 48.4% in 2014, which is the age range in which the data suggests people are most likely to shift their political values and sentiment.

Table 3 | Homeownership rates by age, 2002 to 2014 (%)

Age groups	2002	2006	2010	2014	Change 2002 to 2014
18 – 24	6.2	4.2	4.1	2.4	-3.8
25 – 29	31.0	24.8	27.5	19.9	-11.1
30 – 34	48.5	46.0	45.6	38.7	-9.8
35 – 39	61.0	58.6	57.0	48.4	-12.6
All persons aged 18 - 39	35.7	32.1	31.2	25.2	-10.5

Source: Melbourne Institute of Applied Economic and Social Research, The Household, Income and Labour Dynamics in Australia Survey: selected Findings from Wave 1 to 15, 2017, p. 89.

More disturbing is the list of the subsections of the community that are likely to be over-represented in this trend: couples with dependent children, and those in the second lowest economic quintile, which has experienced drops of 16.8% and 20.5% respectively over the timeframe.[21]

Table 4 | Home-ownership rates by family type, 2002 to 2014 (%)

Family type	2002	2006	2010	2014	Change 2002 to 2014
Couple	46.7	39.9	43.0	35.1	-11.7
Couple with dependent children	55.5	51.2	48.0	38.6	-16.8
Single parent	19.4	18.8	14.2	11.2	-8.2
Single	17.6	17.4	19.1	12.5	-5.1
Non-dependent children	4.4	3.1	3.1	3.6	-0.8

Source: Melbourne Institute of Applied Economic and Social Research, The Household, Income and Labour Dynamics in Australia Survey: selected Findings from Wave 1 to 15, 2017, p. 90.

Table 5 | Home-ownership rates by income quintile, 2002 to 2014 (%)

Income quintile	2002	2006	2010	2014	Change 2002 to 2014
Bottom quintile	19.0	15.4	13.3	12.8	-6.3
2nd quintile	37.0	32.4	26.5	16.6	-20.5
3rd quintile	32.6	34.5	33.2	26.2	-6.3
4th quintile	41.0	37.2	36.0	33.0	-8.1
Top quintile	41.9	34.3	38.6	32.3	-9.6

Source: Melbourne Institute of Applied Economic and Social Research, The Household, Income and Labour Dynamics in Australia Survey: selected Findings from Wave 1 to 15, 2017, p. 90.

The constant increase in the price of housing has made it less affordable for people over time, and notably people's debt levels have continued to rise, as well as their equity ratio. In 2002, the average equity in a home was 57%. By 2014, it had dropped to 42% as the price of housing increased. And amongst new homeowners,[22] the data is even worse: dropping from 42% in 2006 to 34% by 2014.[23] While they are still fortunate to own a home, in practice the cost has only continued to rise and created increasing barriers to entry for those not in the market.

There are numerous factors that directly influence the price of housing, ranging from location to land availability, planning regulations, development and environmental regulations, taxes, savings rates, and access to well-paying jobs. It should hardly surprise anyone that the Australian city with the highest average salaries has the most expensive property market; especially when compounded by factors such as Sydney Harbour.

Distance is a sacrifice many people have to make as a trade-off. A study from Imperial College London found that unless there are significant improvements in transport technology, which increase the capacity for people to live further away from cities, the price of housing will continue to rise.[24] Other factors include technology to improve housing availability through densification in proximity to locations of employment.

Influence of homeownership on political values

Part of the challenge that must be unpacked is the distorted priorities of homeowners. Until people buy their first home, access to affordable housing is of critical importance. The more expensive housing is overall, the higher rents have to be paid while people save a deposit. No one wants higher hurdles for their first foot on the property ladder because it requires a larger deposit, and the discipline required curtails discretionary expenditure. If house prices rise faster than incomes, then the task of homeownership can become insurmountable. Yet once an individual purchases a home for the first time, their concern about rising house prices essentially flips from a concern about ensuring the affordability of purchasing their asset to improving its value and its contributing to their overall wealth. It's then in the interests of owners to increase prices, and keep them high. It isn't just because of the allure of wealth, but also because many people then see the equity in their homes as security for other activities, including small business lending. So dismissing homeowners' interests comes at its own cost.

In 2001, an American professor of economics, William Fischel, developed the Homevoter Hypothesis. It proved what most of us instinctively know: homeowners (like everyone else) act in their own best interests and want to conserve and increase their house prices and will act accordingly. Fischel draws on American evidence to argue that homeowners have a natural interest in supporting tight planning regulations that would limit the use of available land, subdivisions, and developments that would increase supply and suppress prices. Similarly, the direct connection between property values and personal interests leads him to conclude that "residents of owner-occupied homes have a special interest in local affairs that makes local behaviour much different than that of the same actors at the state or national level" where interests are generally in favour of growth and opportunity.[25]

How this translates from the United States to Australia is not clear, but the principles that sit behind it are. While it may not be homeowners' core motivation, homeownership can lead to people consciously opposing housing development in proximity to their own home because an increase in housing is likely to soften prices. There are many other reasons people oppose development: the conservation of their community and neighborhood character, access to infrastructure, including parking and sewage, and population density, as well as simple issues of privacy—few people want multi-storey developments located next to them that overlook their backyard and block light. And that's without discussing the tendency of homeowners in established suburbs, particularly those that are affluent, to have a limited incentive to welcome low-cost housing, especially for younger families and newly arrived migrants; and especially forms of public housing.

Following the recent political upheaval, David Adler and Ben Ansell studied the direct connection between property ownership and the rise of political populism.[26] They concluded that "existing research has completely overlooked the single most important determinant of people's everyday welfare, the largest asset on their household balance sheets, and the driver of massive macroeconomic instability over the last two decades: housing".[27] Adler and Ansell found that voting patterns in the Brexit refendum and France's 2017 presidential election shared a common feature:

> the housing market is closely tied to populist electoral outcomes: areas that have gained from house price inflation are far less likely to vote for populist causes or parties than areas that have been excluded from those gains . . . [and] has a strong effect on populist support independent of these socio-economic and demographic factors . . . [such as] age, income, gender and education.[28]

Critically, they concluded that house prices impact what they term "second dimension" politics,[29] which focuses on inclusion versus exclusion identification, and that when wealth accumulation has been influenced by house prices and improved economic security, the temptation of populism is minimalised.

Homeownership and political preferences

The extent of the divide in attitudes and outlooks led historians Niall Ferguson and Eyck Freymann to warn in *The Atlantic* of "the coming generation war" that they predict, based on the structural imbalances against Millennials. They conclude that "millennials cannot be blamed for concluding that the economy is rigged against them. True, in absolute terms, Americans under 40 carry less debt than middle-aged Americans. But their debt profile is toxic . . . Nearly half of [their debt] comes from student loans and credit cards".[30] This presents a challenge that is now commonly understood—an excessive consumer culture achieved at the expense of saving and the (sometimes indefinite) delay of major life events such as marriage and homeownership.

This data points to a disturbing generational conclusion: if a generation can't secure basic life ambitions and be part of a liberal constituency, then evolution will be of little interest compared to revolution. The data suggests this should be of concern to the Liberal Party as the closest custodian of the Australian liberal tradition. Data from the Australian Electoral Survey reveals a strong correlation between being an owner of property and electoral behaviour. Homeowners are far more likely to vote for the Liberal Party, compared to other parties (including their coalition partner—the Nationals). At the 2019 Federal election, 46% of homeowners voted Liberal, compared to 33% of homeowners who voted Labor with 6% Greens and 4% Nationals (taking the combined Coalition share to 50%), whereas 41% of renters vote Labor, 26% Liberal, 20% Green, and 1% National.[31]

Unsurprisingly, that influence is exacerbated through one of the most financially conservative investment vehicles—property ownership. At the same election, 57% of investment property owners vote Liberal, 27% Labor, 7% Green and 2% National (taking the combined Coalition share to 59%). Of those who do not own an investment property, 37% vote Labor, 36% Liberal, 13% Green and 3% National.

Table 6 | Home ownership outright or with mortgage per Federal electorate[a]

Bottom 10	Owner rate (%)	Party held	2PP vote (%)	Primary vote (%)
Sydney	26.72	Labor	68.67	49.41
Melbourne	27.94	Greens	71.83	49.30
Lingiari	32.45	Labor	55.46	44.80
Durack	34.86	Liberal	64.76	44.30
Macnamara[b]	35.36	Labor	56.25	31.78
Brisbane	37.53	LNP	54.92	47.84
Solomon	38.37	Labor	53.08	40.04
Wentworth	42.24	Liberal	51.31	47.44
Parramatta	42.52	Labor	53.5	45.08
Griffith	42.67	Labor	52.86	30.95
Top 10	**Owner rate (%)**	**Party held**	**2PP vote (%)**	**Primary vote (%)**
Berowra	74.74	Liberal	65.65	57.20
Hughes	73.89	Liberal	59.85	53.16
Mitchell	72.62	Liberal	68.63	62.05
La Trobe	72.60	Liberal	54.49	45.72
Moore	72.01	Liberal	61.65	51.25
Casey	71.43	Liberal	54.64	45.25
Menzies	70.19	Liberal	57.53	51.73
Aston	69.74	Liberal	60.13	54.69
Cowan	69.36	Labor	50.83	38.13
Dickson	67.68	LNP	54.64	45.93

Source: Australian Electoral Commission data, Census data.

Home ownership rates based on Australian Bureau of Statistics 2016 Census Data
Election results based on 2019 Federal election data
[a] Between the Census data and 2019 election electorates were redistributed
[b] formerly Melbourne Ports

The electoral data on homeownership rates in electorates held by different parties reinforces the correlation. The ten electorates with the lowest marital rates nearly mirror those of homeownership rates. There are, of course, parallels between the two. Low marital rates increase the chance that an individual is saving a deposit for a home alone. Wentworth is an outlier and reflects an established community with high property prices and a younger overall demographic, akin to electorates such as Brisbane, Melbourne, and Sydney as capital cities, as well as electorates neighbouring capitals, such as Macnamara to the inner south of Melbourne. And the top ten electorates for home ownership are also completely dominated by Liberal electorates that are all suburban or outer-suburban, where house prices are more affordable, and many bring with them hefty electoral margins. The outlier is the federal electorate of Cowan, in the inner-north of Perth, which has a low primary vote and a low two-party preferred vote.

Correlation isn't causation. There are other indicators that affect sentiments likely to influence voting behaviour. As we demonstrated earlier, age is resolutely one, as can be gender. Looking at electoral returns, there's also a clear correlation between marital rates and the likelihood of voting behaviour. Those with the highest marital rates are all Liberal-held seats, bar one, which has traditionally been Liberal-held.[32] The difference between these factors and housing is the capacity for public policy to influence outcomes. Public policy can only indirectly affect ageing, can do little on a person's gender and has exhausted its options in enlarging the franchise for civil marriage; whereas public policy can have a direct impact on homeownership—positive or negative.

Unaffordable housing and the threat to liberalism

This data should concern any liberal, not just because it raises questions about the political constituency for those who want to apply liberalism practically, but also because it raises structural questions about an open economy and society and the freedom for social mobility.

As home prices have risen, there has been a narrowing of those who can access the market independently. Rising prices have led to a higher number of Australians requiring the assistance of family members to assist them in making their first step into the property market. In 2019, Genworth found in a study of almost 3,000 first homebuyers that "almost seven in 10 (68.7%) . . . reported that they did not fund 100% of their deposit from their own savings, with the majority (56.9%) relying on parental or family assistance".[33] Other studies from the same year have found the number to be around 20%,[34] and the Reserve Bank of Australia has found those relying on loans, not grants and gifts from parents or family members, to be even lower, but increasing year-on-year.[35] Such data is unlikely to be reliable, as many applicants for mortgages do not disclose in their applications additional sources of financial support, on the basis that it can limit their access to finance if they're seen not to be good savers, or potentially carry a debt to parents or family.

Australian Housing and Urban Research Institute data found intergenerational wealth transfer to secure housing has broader socio-economic impacts than simply getting individuals into the market. It concluded that "intergenerational transfers impact on housing outcomes for first-time buyers along at least two dimensions. First, as noted, they tend to accelerate transitions into the ownership tenure;

second, they tend to increase the amount paid for housing rather than being used to limit the size of the loan taken out".[36]

In the past thirty years, the opportunity for wealth creation has evened out as a consequence of compulsory superannuation. But homeownership remains the primary vehicle for wealth storage and accumulation. The family home is Australians' single largest asset at around $500,000, and more than double the average value of Australians' second largest asset, superannuation at just over $210,000.[37] That has political consequences. With a foothold in the market, people's wealth can increase with marginal consequence to their own productivity or contribution beyond financing debt. Critically, because of the preferential taxation associated with the family home, it encourages more and more of the nation's scarce capital into an economically inefficient asset—it is slow and complex to trade, it stores significant capital that could be put towards a growth-orientated productive purpose, and it limits disposable income.

But the more substantial concern should be what it is doing to the very structure of the social contract. The primary vehicle through which Australians accumulate and hold wealth is property, and with more Australians relying on their parents to assist them to secure their first property, the risk is that property ownership is increasingly dependent on your parent's assets. Yet the foundation of the modern Australian social contract is to break the mould of hereditary privilege that was present in Europe, in favour of a more open and democraticised social contract of individuals owning homes and engaging in enterprise.

8

Big community, not Canberra

The failure of centralised power

What makes liberalism distinct from all other political philosophies is that it doesn't pursue power for the sake of some abstract objective, such as equity or order.

The ultimate form of decentralisation is the individual. Individuals represent the most independent agency in human affairs. The importance of decentralised power to the individual ultimately makes it a threat to political ideologies that inevitably end in centralising power. Their solution has sometimes been substitution and at other times suffocation. The concept of individual rights came from the Western liberal tradition. Following the atrocities of the Second World War, countries worked to established international treaties to instill the concept of 'human rights' to act as a bulwark against future oppression. Debates surrounding the Universal Declaration of Human Rights and the International Covenant on Civil and Political Rights divided along the lines of collectivist socialist centralist ideas of rights and the individual liberal decentralist alternative. In his history of the International Covenant on Civil and Political Rights, the Austrian human rights lawyer, Manfred Nowak, wrote about how Articles 19 and 20 (the Articles supporting freedom of thought and expression) demonstrated the tension:

> the liberal view, every individual has the freedom to form his or her own opinions free from external indoctrination and to defend them in the "free market of ideas" without fear of repression . . . The zone of legitimate State intervention commences at the point where the expression of an opinion interferes with the rights of others or constitutes an obvious, direct threat to life in society . . . [whereas] according to the socialist view, human rights are, in general, the embodiment of the very essence of the Socialist State and are marked by an "objective conformity of interests between the citizen and the socialist society freed of class antagonism".[1]

In essence, freedom of speech was entirely consistent with the socialist worldview—so long as it wasn't disruptive to conformity. One of the many reasons that a free press falls prey to centralist regimes is because it promotes subversive accountability and challenges the ambition of conformity propagated by the state.

Similarly, family, religion, civil society, and other alternative forms of competitive organization and authority necessarily become a target of a centralised state—to be maligned, corrupted through dependence on government through sponsorship, or banned. And decentralisation of political power is no different. Even where there is administrative or fiscal decentralisation, it is normally tied to the permission and oversight from the central authority, with a limited freedom for divergence.

To have a liberal society for individuals necessitates some form of centralised framework of rules to foster stability through peace and order, national security and independent justice, peaceful trade, and the protection of property so individuals can enjoy their life, liberty, and the pursuit of happiness. No matter the size of the government, there is necessarily some bureaucracy to bring about the programs of government. By its nature, bureaucracy involves centralised authority seeking to impose uniform measures across society and the economy.

Overcoming centralisation

Empowerment of a centralised bureaucracy will always be in tension with empowered individuals, because it must take some freedom and responsibility (and tax) from the individual to implement uniform solutions. Bureaucracy is designed to manage 'a people', but not for individuals. It is why smaller government is an essential pursuit in order for individuals to flourish. If a government agency can make decisions over people's lives, direct their choices, or take responsibility, it can only be in place of the choices that individuals would make for themselves.

Other liberal pursuits necessitate government to tax and distribute some of the value of property to create an environment of equality of opportunity to fund quality education and health services (which partly undo the injustices bestowed on individuals by nature such, as indiscriminate diseases of birth). Understanding the liberal solution also depends on understanding how best to address these problems. A socialist would look at the problems of health and education and conclude that the best method for addressing issues of inequity is through publicly financed and operated services. A liberal would look at how a diversity of private organizations could provide them in a competitive environment, the role that the taxpayer has to play in addressing issues of access, and the responsibility of the individual.

As outlined in Chapter 6, the individual's family and their home encapsulate the individual's autonomy and self-reliance, and are the manifestation of the individual's economic, social, and cultural independence. The strength of the community and the country is linked back directly to the health of individuals, and by extension their families. Decentralisation drives competition between multiple sources of power as a means of driving progress. As Hayek argues in *The Road to Serfdom*:

> The liberal argument does not advocate leaving things just as they are; it favours making the best possible use of the forces of competition as a means of coordinating human efforts. It is based on the conviction that, where effective competition can be created, it is a better way of guiding individual efforts than any other.[2]

The institutions that are a realisation of that empowerment are many and varied—the ballot, civil liberties, a free press with a contest of competitive ideas to drive progress and innovation and fundamental freedoms for political power, deregulated and competitive price signals, competition and ownership for economic power, and the family and voluntary community-based civil society, and faith-based organizations for social and cultural power. Each of these directly contradicts identity and group rights, centralised bureaucracies, corporatist and union might, and collective identity (though religion and nationalism can create alternative competing authorities depending on their forms, such as cultural or moral authority that rests with hierarchical churches, or ethnic community authorities that defer to home nations). And in governance, decentralisation of proximate and accountable authorities to individuals, communities, and regional governance provides a check on power, as does the separation of powers between the legislature, judiciary, and executive to deliver accountability, rather than a monopoly that reserves the right to use violence to enforce its will against non-compliance: government.

There is a dramatic divide within Western liberal democratic societies between those who are essentially proximate to the power of centralised institutions—governments, corporates, and cultural institutions, including universities and the media—and the rest of the population. That large and expanding divide ensures that levels of trust can only go in one direction, leading people to the conclusion that these institutions no longer reflect their interests. If individuals can't affect an institution that is broadly designed to reflect or address their interests, they face three choices: seek to influence it to make it more reflective; walk away from it if they can't influence it; or break it, if they can't walk away from it but want to do so, and then rebuild it according to their interests. In the United Kingdom, people walked away from the European Union. In the United States, after initially trying to influence Washington DC through the rise of the anti-government Tea Party movement after the Global Financial Crisis, some Americans were ultimately left with few choices when they could not bring about the change they sought. Ultimately, they elected someone who spoke to the idea of breaking a national capital that could not be reined in under the banner of "draining the swamp".

Increasing proximity to power

This rarely happens at a local level; frustration and anger rarely build up to the level at which there are demands to smash institutions in order to bring about change. When people are unhappy with the service they receive from a business, they simply shop at a competitor. If they are unhappy with the offerings of a local cultural institution, they stop buying tickets or donating money. And if they are not happy with the performance of their local council, they change their councilors. There is no need to change the institution itself. Proximity to effect change matters. As does accountability to effect change, which includes ensuring that people who have responsibility can be held to account. In the European Union, the British representatives can say what they want, but unelected Commissioners have influence and the French and Germans are easy scapegoats for failing to effect reform. Unlike most Congressmen and women, the buck always stops with the President.

The Economist magazine devoted a special issue to rediscovering the importance of the traditions and strengths of open societies for a modern context. Today, societies seem so open that, in order to regain some form of control, the certainty that can be achieved by reversing the tide and closing the economy or society to pursue security seems irresistible. It is misplaced. Closure is not needed for control. Instead, we need to return to a way of life in which society, the economy, and governance are built from citizens and communities rather than from capital city elites and centalised authority. In one essay in this special issue, "Some thoughts on the crisis of liberalism – and how to fix it", *The Economist's* Bagehot column argues:

> liberalism as a philosophy has been captured by a technocratic-managerial-cosmopolitan elite. A creed that started off as a critique

of the existing power structure—that, indeed has suspicion of concentrations of power at the molten core of its philosophy—is being misused as a tool by one of the most powerful elites in history. Liberalism has, in effect been turned on its head and become the opposite of what it was when it started out.[3]

The rise of populism has partly come from the increasing centralisation of power. Bagehot writes that "by insulating technocratic elites from the pressure of popular opinion—by putting them in a comfortable cocoon of like-minded elites—it encourages over-reach".[4] This is the ultimate cocoon of the 'Anywheres', 'Inners' and 'SuperZips' of Chapter 4; people who have never met someone who disagrees with them on a range of issues; people who view life simply from a position of privilege and focus on the challenges of prosperity. Worse, the drift of power through managerialism from individuals to national governments reduces accountability which is only exacerbated further through international institutions and multinational corporations that leverage economic efficiency.

The argument so often made in favour of centralisation is the efficiency and the utility of trusting experts. Both concepts are now synonymous with public policy development. As a Member of Parliament, there is no end to the number of lobbyists who use either of these, as well as the benefit to the budget, as a justification for their desired public policy outcome. All three are worthy goals, but all lack a connection to a human understanding of politics, or, my retort to lobbyists: "MPs don't go in to bat for budget savings. Bureaucrats do that. Convince me it is the right thing to do." Yet the logical argument for those who seek to influence centralised power is to appeal to the central authority's interests. As Bagehot observes:

the biggest problem with managerialism, however is not that it is inefficient but that it divides humanity into two classes of people: the rulers and the ruled, the doers and the done to, the thinkers and the hood-carriers. It recreates the very division that liberals, in their salad days, set out to destroy—though this time the people at the top are a global elite of educated citizens, wearing their MBAs like modern coat of arms, and the people at the bottom are the uneducated masses, condemned to spend their lives on the received end of orders.[5]

To draw from the Maslow hierarchy, they have the foundations to focus on post-materialist self-actualisation to broaden their perspective beyond themselves. Their focus is on the implementation of distribution channels and capital raising and systems of government of how to design the pegs that individuals fit in. What they forget— or never knew—is what it is like to be an individual peg. Not every individual peg fits in a round hole. What they have lost connection to, or take for granted, are the basic needs of housing, food, water, employment, and health, and draw security from proximity to others in like circumstances. Critically, national identity anchors individuals and provides security around common bonds that breed a necessary pre-condition for the operation of a liberal order: trust.

Technocracy is the tyranny of feudalism revisited: unelected, unaccountable, and viewing humanity through the lens of automatons without agency. Technocracy and managerialism are also directly connected to the shortcomings of liberal internationalism. Liberal internationalism is actually quite illiberal. It is a reflection of the empowerment of governments, not individuals. It seeks to centralise ideals away from individuals to pursue international universal aims. The only way they can be achieved is through the empowerment of international centralised authority. The experience of humanity to date is that international institutions do not take account of local contexts and cannot be truly democratic. Furthermore, the proximity required for individuals to hold international bodies accountable or to effect change in them is nearly non-existent. As de Tocqueville observed, "from a general, higher viewpoint, patriotism, despite its great impulses and deeds, would seem a false and narrow passion . . . the interests of the human race are better served by giving every man a particular fatherland than by trying to inflame his passions for the whole of humanity".[6]

These are not just issues of governance, but also of economics. In its handbook for policymakers, *Making Decentralisation Work*, the OECD highlights the emergence of "a 'geography of discontent' and growing divides between places that feel left behind by globalisation and technological change".[7] There are many reasons why decentralisation can aid in addressing the perception of a 'geography of discontent', but one of the most important "is a positive association with decentralisation and political participation" and "fiscal decentralisation and citizen participation".[8]

Addressing populism

To this end, in 2018, the former Conservative Canadian prime minister, Stephen Harper, wrote *Right Here, Right Now: Politics and Leadership in the Age of Disruption*, a book reflecting on recent events including the success of the referendum that led to Brexit and the election of Donald Trump. Harper's analysis reassesses the challenges facing liberal democracies, particularly in response to global economic integration, so that their contribution to the rise of populism can be properly confronted. Harper picks up the themes that are covered in Murray and Goodhart's analysis, when he explains that "there is a widening chasm between the perspectives of establishment institutions of all kinds—corporations, banks, bureaucracies, academia, media, entertainment—and those who do not identify with such institutions".[9] Governments and institutions must be connected with, and reflect, people's lives, because "you have some responsibility as a citizen to be somewhere. And if you do not understand that, then you will behave as if you have no responsibilities at all".[10] Harper laments the fact that, when people have a disconnect from the institutions that are designed to serve those people, they seek out populism regardless of their background, because:

> Populism is a framework for identifying political priorities and making political decisions. But it does not tell us much about the underlying policies per se. So-called populist politicians have stood for ideas that could be classed as left-wing, right-wing, or even centrist.[11]

And therefore:

> the solution to the excesses of globalism is not a top-down, all-knowing, centralised nation-state. That would just substitute distant bureaucratic decisions with slightly closer, yet still distant, bureaucratic decisions. This is why conservatives need to support a positive role for civil society and localism as well.[12]

The evidence base is clear. The cost of disconnected institutions to the lives of people led to:

> the twin phenomena of Bernie Sanders and Donald Trump. Their agendas may have been diametrically different, but there was something common in their appeal. How else do you explain the Sanders-Trump 'switcher'? About 12 per cent of Sanders supporters in the Democratic Primary cross over to Trump in the general election. In several key states—Pennsylvania, Wisconsin and Michigan—the number of Sanders-to-Trump defectors was greater than Trump's margin of victory.[13]

Harper is half right. Sanders and Trump were not as diametrically opposed as logic might suggest. It's certainly true that Sanders wants to turn the United States socialist and would be easily identified on the 'left' of the political spectrum. But it is hard to suggest that Trump is really the exact opposite. Sanders wants to put the material improvement of the welfare of Americans first, and wants to use the state to achieve that purpose. While cloaking himself in the banner of the Republican Party, in truth Trump is closer to being an old school industrialist who also wants to improve the welfare of Americans. Trump isn't necessarily left-wing. But both Trump and Sanders essentially speak to the material improvement of the average American. Both Trump and Sanders speak to Americans who feel left behind, and who yearn for a sense of justice in the world: Sanders through government; Trump through commerce.

No one would describe Trump as a traditional Republican, even if you think he still fits within the spectrum of Republicanism. In truth, Trump's values appear to be a closer reflection of a 'Copper Head Democrat'—and not just because of his complexion. Copper Head Democrats were a tradition of New Yorkers who sided with the South during the Civil War. They were industrialist, commercial-minded, and mercantilist, but operated under the banner of a form of nationalism that is back in vogue as a backlash against globalism.

Increasing individuals' influence

In his rebuke of Donald Trump, on the eve of his election as President of the United States, the American conservative icon, William Kristol, called for the American conservative movement "to preserve and strengthen American liberal democracy . . . a conservatism based on old conservative—and liberal—principles".[14] Of course, the wordplay on what is meant by liberalism and conservatism in the American tradition can lead to a situation in which Americans would be uncomfortable jumping between the two. Ofir Haivry and Yoram Hazony, of the Herzl Institute in Jerusalem, write in an essay on "What is Conservatism?" in the journal, *American Affairs*, that the relationship between classical liberalism and conservatism has traditionally been strong: "among the effects of the long alliance between conservatism and [classical] liberalism has been a tendency of political figures, journalists, and academics to slip back and forth between conservative terms and ideas and liberal ones as if they were interchangeable".[15] Though they warn that the "lack of clarity [of understanding about the two] is crippling our ability to think about a host of issues" because American conservatism has its roots in classical liberalism.[16] They argue that this tradition includes five fundamental principles:

- historical empiricism based upon "constitutional traditions, known through the long historical experience for a given nation to offer stability, well-being and freedom";

- nationalism due to "unity anchored in common traditional law and religion" [and] "not based on race";

- religion that is "indispensable for justice and public morals" coupled with "religious and social views that do not endanger the integrity and well-being of the nation as a whole";

- executive power limited by "the representatives of the people, whose advice and consent [they] must obtain both respecting the laws and taxation"; and

- individual freedoms that "may be infringed upon only by due process of law".[17]

In essence, this is the liberal understanding of anchoring power that affects individuals in the institutions located closest to them, and this proximity is achieved through proximate feedback loops.

If you do not have feedback loops, you can't adjust and be responsive. In an age of hyper-empowered consumers who have choice, but also the capacity to broadcast their views and build communities of interest based on them, the need to be nimble only increases the need to be responsive and reflective. Liberalism has always understood the power of feedback loops. It understands that the biggest threat to liberty comes from the coercive hand of government, which can impose its will with only the limited accountability of distant electoral cycles. The marketplace, in contrast to the hand of government, is accountable to the proximate and daily market signals.

Local communities and local decisions

Despite the global integration resulting from technology and travel, the vast majority of most individuals' lives remain geographically local. They grow up, work, and live within the same city or country. People travel. Through Facebook, they may occasionally 'like' the photo a friend posted on social media; a friend whom they may only have caught up with once through a postcard or as a pen pal. But otherwise, individuals' lives are still dominated by their immediate surrounds and the stages of life they walk through: parent-teacher nights at school, paying the mortgage, office politics, and worrying about financial security in retirement. They voice their judgement on their elected officials at the ballot box every few years. They would frankly prefer these officials understood their stresses better, and focused on getting on with the job rather than fighting amongst themselves. It is the peculiarity of being Australian: we enjoy much, so we do not expect heroism. If we can all get on with our job, then, surely, we can expect politicians to do the same.

The irony is that when something goes wrong, we love having someone to blame. Complaining about too many government agencies is a throwaway barbecue debating point. The council should just focus on picking up the rubbish. No one really knows what States do anymore, except maybe run the trains, hospitals, and schools, and that they always seem to be underfunded by Canberra. The prevailing sentiment is that anything serious is done in Canberra. They are the ones on the TV on the evening news, after all. They have bigger personalities and our tax dollars to go with it. The logic is that the solution is to abolish the States and make everything faster, cheaper, and consistent.

In his book, *The Demons of Liberal Democracy*, British professor of politics, Adrian Pabst, argues that it is this disconnect of proximity that is causing upheaval within liberal democracy. He argues, consistently with Murray, that "it was not just their marginalisation in the economy that voters resented. The fact that they voted against their economic self-interest suggests that their revulsion was to do with the denigration of their values and identities by the members of the professional political class".[18]

Pabst argues correctly that the challenges plaguing liberal democracy are often the byproduct of a liberalism unanchored from society. He writes:

> liberalism is a slippery term with many meanings . . . [and] what
> has failed is not the whole tradition, but, rather, a contemporary
> radicalisation of specific ideals, in particular (1) freedom without
> social solidarity (going back to John Locke and Immanuel Kant); (2)

the primacy of the individual underwritten by the collective power of the state over civic associations (going back to Thomas Hobbes and Jean-Jacques Rousseau); and (3) faith in a better future underpinned by a secular metaphysics of progress (going back to Auguste Comte and J. S. Mill).[19]

Much of that disconnect is not just a direct consequence of different values, but also of different lives driven by geographic separation between people living urban, regional, and rural lives, each of which bring with them their own source of identity.

Australian's relationship with banks is a clear example. Banks always had headquarters where men in bowler hats had an orderly and prudent existence, but outside of cashing a cheque on a visit to 'town', most people engaged with their local branch, clerks, and managers. Progressively, that declined. Branches closed—and despite how it is often perceived—mostly because people didn't need them anymore. It was just easier to go online to transfer money and manage your finances. With technology, deposits and withdrawals could be done through an ATM or a post office. More complex products like mortgages or investing needed other avenues, but their infrequency meant a higher degree of centralisation in regional offices was viable.

As branches closed, proximity declined. Locals no longer knew their branch manager and a relationship built on trust progressively shifted to one based on evidence. Local knowledge went. And the people in local bank branches, who reflected the values of the community, were no longer there. The values of the bank were now connected to the head office. Everything local was severed for the benefit of scale. The non-financial equity of the bank declined. And if you had a problem, the best you could do is complain to a phone line. Relationships go. Trust goes. Choice can also go. It does not mean the decision is wrong. But it does mean the decision has consequences. And when compounded with government, the economy, and culture, the proximity divide seems wide.

Addressing the challenge involves connecting individuals' ambitions back to their model of governance, and seeing how their lives are lived through institutions designed to serve them:

> key to the success of renewed regional autonomy is to reconnect urban spaces to their rural surroundings wherever possible and thereby to break down the existing barriers and to rebalance the priorities away from urban and metropolitan towards suburban and rural areas. Regional representation requires not just proper constitutional recognition and political status. The crucial point is that regions, big or small, refract particular identities often with deep historical roots, for example counties in England. People do not feel any attachment to the North West, the North east or the South East, which were always artificial entities, but they have great affection for Yorkshire, Kent or Surrey.[20]

The solution isn't just about closing physical distance, but fiscal distance as well. A 2011 study showed that an increase in fiscal decentralisation equates to an improvement in trust in government and "the beneficial effect of fiscal decentralisation on trust in government is neither limited to nor necessarily large for relatively decentralised countries".[21] Basically, the improvements occur regardless of the degree of pre-existing decentralisation. No matter how little or how much a state is centralised, empowering its citizens and communities will always build trust in government compared with empowerment of centralised capitals. As the OECD has stated, decentralisation also improves political stability:

decentralising powers to regions and subnational governments, the tensions arising due to various cultural, historical or political reasons may be mitigated. This can also happen because decentralisation might be asymmetric, thus making it easier to take into account certain territorial specificities . . . [and] since decentralisation generates a larger number of political arenas and government layers (compared with a centralised model), pressure on candidates to win elections at the national level at any cost may be diminished.[22]

Similarly, a study from the Shanghai University of Finance and Economics found:

When decision-making authority is devolved to lower level of government, citizens are provided with more incentives and opportunities to become engaged in the policy making process. In particular, local constituents are more motivated to participate in decision making because they are better informed about local affairs and that local affairs are more related to their interests.[23]

As with all concentrations of power, the challenge for liberals is around the parameters of when the advantages of concentrating power—ranging from efficiency to a capacity to leverage for future investments and collaboration—outweigh the risk of becoming predatory and undermining competition. The greater the democractisation of the economic wealth of the nation, which is accessible through an open economy, the greater the number of citizens who have the opportunity to earn and secure it. And the greater the number that share in the prosperity of the nation, the deeper their stake and interest in a country's future is. As Kemp explains:

A number of political movements in the nineteenth century were inspired by the dream of a classless society—not only the Australian liberals but also socialist, communist and even anarchist movements.

These movements differ partly in what they meant by classlessness, but their differences primarily lay in their assessment of how to dismantle the old order . . . Liberals saw the road to a classless society through the promotion of an egalitarian democratic culture, broadening the ownership of private property, universal education and politics that secured the equal freedom of all to pursue their own goals in life.[24]

Economic benefits of decentralisation

If a centrally planned economy were to compete against a competitive open market economy, history shows that the one delivers bread lines and the other abundance. A central planner can never have the necessary knowledge to understand the changing demands of individuals. Even an inventory of the consumption of a household at a snapshot in time is useless for replication as people's lives and circumstances change. Whereas decentralised information through price signals creates ripple effects across the whole of the economy to unintentionally guide market behaviour for goods and services: what should be produced, the demand for it, the resources required to produce it—including investment costs as well as the value of physical and intellectual property, the speed of its delivery and the cost of waste generated. Concurrently, all these factors incentivise competition and innovation that only serve to increase the economic power of the individual. Profits are inherently linked to meeting market demand and are as tenuous as the longevity of that relationship. Economic transactions are also blind to prejudice with only price signals guiding decision-making. It is why free markets have always been tied to social progress. Economic empowerment builds security for those traditionally oppressed and trade prompts engagement between people regardless of their background, building mutual awareness and respect. The reverse is true in central planning and collective ownership. The incentives and diffuse knowledge are lost and the profits are secured by the producer regardless. There are many good economic arguments around the efficient use of capital and resources to justify private property and free enterprise, but its enduring strength is the economic decentralisation of economic power from the hands of the few to the potential of every individual.

The misunderstanding is that decentralisation of economic or political power leaves individuals as islands alone and isolated; left to defend themselves against those with greater power in a predatory dog-eat-dog world. That interpretation is wrongheaded about the true threat to empowerment. The misunderstanding reflects a centralist worldview that, by imposing conformity, our society and economy can be designed to manage the interests of others, and to ensure that people are not taken advantage of. It also takes no account of the likelihood that centralised authority carries risk of abuse!

What it does not take account of is the capacity for individuals to have complex and individual needs; needs that cannot all be satisfied in isolation. If people lived in isolation, they'd spend most of their day engaging in the basic activities necessary to ensure they had a nourishing breakfast: seeding and tilling fields, growing crops, collecting firewood, and mining for the minerals to make a pan. And, in doing so, their existence would never transcend beyond subsistence. It is because individuals saw themselves as capable beyond their own isolation that they have progressed and succeeded. Through the division of labour and the trade of goods and services, we have gone from subsistence living to the most complex and dynamic economic system that has ever existed. Individuals pursuing their own interests necessarily fosters mutual dependence as a means of achieving those interests. It is through the pursuit of voluntary interactions and exchange in the marketplace that individuals advance not only their aims, but those of others. The bigger risk today is not that individuals are islands, but that their interconnectedness poses its own risks through over-dependence on highly integrated supply chains and modern finance. Whatever the shortcomings of sophisticated, overly complex systems are, they can only evolve organically. Their organic development allows for constant signals to adjust and make them sustainable. Central authorities cannot replicate them. Only the voluntary cooperation of millions of empowered individuals could do so.

Social benefits of decentralisation

The power of pursuing a society ordered from the individual citizen is the social harmony and civility that comes through voluntary interaction. This was a common theme in Adam Smith's works, in which he argues that cooperation promotes civil interactions in the marketplace and civil society. He writes:

> All the members of human society stand in need of each other's assistance, and are likewise exposed to mutual injuries. Where the necessary assistance is reciprocally afforded from love, from gratitude, from friendship and esteem, the society flourishes and is happy. All the different members of it are bound together by agreeable bonds of love and affection, and are, as it were, drawn to one common centre of mutual good offices.[25]

The British minister of state and Conservative Member of Parliament, Jesse Norman, describes the long tradition of the civilising force of voluntary action between free people in his book, *Adam Smith: What he thought and why it matters*. He explains that "A core purpose of *The Theory of Moral Sentiments* is, by explaining how moral feelings arise from human sociability, to vindicate the claims of civilization itself as a force for more improvement".[26] He continues:

> Smith underlines the social dimension of individual self-consciousness by considering someone cut off from society altogether: Were it possible that a human creature could grow up to manhood in some solitary place, without any communication with his own species, he could not more think of his own character, of the propriety or demerit of his mind, than of the beauty or deformity of his own face. To have a self, to be self-conscious or self-aware, to draw on social and moral values or exercise judgement in relation to ourselves, thus always involves what Smith calls 'an immediate reference to the sentiments of others'.[27]

The only sustainable solution is to reinvigorate decentralisation in a way that addresses the problem of declining confidence, trust, and proximity caused by centralisation. And for Australia that means going back to our modern roots.

In favour of federalism

The decentralisation of power in the Australian political tradition was not an accident. When Europeans first arrived, they were presented with a continent upon which they sought to build appropriate structures of governance. They recognised the strengths and shortcomings of other systems of government, notably those of the United Kingdom and United States, and adapted them to local conditions.

Instead, they embraced a hybrid of the British Westminster and American Washington models—or Washminster system of government—that included a federal system of the distribution of power that directly rebuffed centralism. As Kemp explains in *A Free Country: Australia's search for utopia 1861-1901*:

> The objective of replacing the liberal economy with a corporatist version required that government authority should be centralised rather than dispersed to maximise the capacity to re-engineer the industrial system. This was often supported by Bellamy-like[*] belief in the efficiency and productiveness of centralisation. A change to the structure of government in the direction of unification of all authority in one set of institutions made its appearance in the labour program after Federation, and to a sustained campaign to delegitimise the devolution inherent in the 1901 Constitution, bas as it was around the deliberate decentralisation of governmental power and the division of sovereignty or authority between the levels of government.[28]

Democracy is a strong expression of the decentralisation of power. In its purest form, direct democracy is the ultimate form of individual political empowerment in a community. Representative democracy is a tempered alternative, which recognises the practical necessity for government with a mechanism for accountability. Representatives chosen by different communities, and meeting in a national capital, will always have to bargain with other representatives who have different concerns and therefore decisions will be broad in their focus, distant in their proximity, bland in their uniformity, and slow in their making. By comparison, localised decision-making will always be more reflective of community values, responsive to shifting community sentiment, and more precise in its capacity to address local circumstances.

---

[*] Edward Bellamy was an American socialist who wrote *Looking Backward 2000-1887*, which argued for centralisation of political and economic power on the basis of efficiency against the alternative inefficiency of decentralisation, which was a direct departure from the earlier Australian Labourist position of accepting the earlier liberal consensus.

In his reflections on the structure of the Commonwealth, Sir Robert Menzies extols the necessity of divided power to defend the liberal democratic ideal because "in the division of power, in the demarcation of powers between a central government and the State governments, there resides one of the true protections of individual freedom".[29] Competitive federalism provides a bulwark against monopoly government through structural accountability, as does the ballot box.

Federation was a celebration of a core liberal ideal—that power should rest closest to the individuals it serves. It created a democratic order that understands that the legitimacy of government comes from individuals. Kemp concludes:

> The task of writing a Constitution for the new nation was nevertheless to raise all the dilemmas inherent in liberalism: the appropriate balance between the rights of minorities and the ultimate power of the majority; the balance between the decentralisation of power and the sovereignty of people; the balance between liberty and democracy, between personal and economic liberty, and the way in which the current passionate debate over the role of government was to be resolved.[30]

Consequently, the ideas of democratic liberalism are infused in the Constitution. It prevents the Commonwealth from restricting freedom of conscience and the practice of religion (though the States can do so), affords protection for private property and compensation for confiscation, and insists upon free trade between the States, the separation of powers, and competitive federalism. The Constitution Act establishes the Commonwealth of Australia, but doesn't seek to determine the direction of democratic decision-making. It provides for the institutions necessary to ensure the new country respects individuals and their freedom, but it leaves ongoing debates about the limits of the state and individuals' relationship to one another as a matter for democratic debate (unlike the rigidity of the American Bill of Rights). Liberal democracy was to be a constant conversation with wide boundaries, not rigid rights-based individualism.

Alas, we are heading in the wrong direction. In 2007, the Council for the Australian Federation commissioned a report on the state of Australia's federation. The report concluded that the federation was "under attack", and that "centralism appears to be the order of the day".[31] The authors found:

> Recent trends in Australian federalism show a shift from competitive and co-operative federalism to a system of 'opportunistic federalism', where the Commonwealth uses its array of financial and legislative powers to intervene selectively in areas of traditional State responsibility to make ideological or political points. In doing so, the Commonwealth undermines the benefits of federalism and exacerbates problems such as duplication and excessive administrative burdens.[32]

Of course, this isn't a recent trend. The decision of the High Court to validate the centralisation of income tax powers from the States to the Commonwealth during the Second World War was the greatest act of fiscal centralisation in Australian history. That decision remains devastating for competitive federalism and the accountability it has placed on taxation across the Commonwealth. When income taxes were set by the States, competition kept the tax burden on individuals low, as individuals could pick the tax jurisdiction of their choice. There was also a greater obligation to justify tax rates and to secure consent for increasing them. The vertical fiscal imbalance that now leads to the Commonwealth raising more funds than it spends, and then using those funds to provide tied grants to the States, has led to more disconnected decisions made in Canberra, anemic States no longer prepared to take fiscal responsibility for their problems, and a culture of blame and buck-passing.

The solution is to recognise that a necessary precondition of a system of political and economic order must always be structured to serve individuals pursuing interests in the narrow sense for themselves, or more broadly through voluntary cooperation in matters that they cannot resolve for themselves—as people do by forming enterprise and community organizations. That is not very liberal, or conservative. So the liberal solution must be to address that gap. That is what former British prime minster, David Cameron, sought to do through the evolution of the concept of the 'Big Society'.

The big society

The Cameron narrative of a 'Big Society' achieved two purposes. The first was to distance the Conservative Party he led from an oft-repeated derisory quote from former British prime minister, Margaret Thatcher. She is quoted as having once said that "there is no such thing as society". This distorts what she meant, however, by taking the quote out of context.[33] Cameron wanted to reassert the idea that he understood there was society as an extension of individuals who form families, and who also form common bonds beyond the household. He wanted to communicate there was a big society. Cameron also wanted to address the fundamental problem that centralised bureaucracy and policy design lacked local considerations in development, and knowledge in rolling out government programmes. Through the 'Big Society', Westminster sought to roll out programmes through community-based organizations, civil society, and local administrations who could take the policy intent and implement it in a reflective way that better met local needs.

In 2010, the British coalition government's plans included a strong decentralisation agenda arguing, "this is a time for a fundamental shift of power from Westminster to people".[34] It fit in with the 'Big Society' narrative run by David Cameron in his agenda for reform of the Conservative Party, and for reform of the United Kingdom. It focused on devolution of power, promoting volunteerism, the promotion of non-profits, and improving government transparency. Critically, it focused on political decentralisation, but not fiscal decentralisation. Ultimately, Cameron wanted to make local and regional entities responsible, but with purse strings tied back to Westminster.

Cameron spoke of the Big Society as a "social recovery" to complement the economic recovery the nation needed after the global financial crisis.[35] It was proposed as a means of promoting local independence and the resurgence of traumatised communities. He said that, unlike the economic recovery that was born out of the need to respond to a major economic event, the social recovery reflected a broader trend of "broken families", "communities breaking down", "the level of crime", "the level of gang membership", "people stuck on welfare, unable to work" and "public services [that] don't work for us". The solution to these problems was articulated in terms of "responsibility". But responsibility isn't just about the idea of ownership; it is also about proximity.

Consistent with the objectives of decentralisation, accountability, and responsiveness, liberals should strongly believe not just in small government, but big citizens and society as well. Not just because they are the realisation of liberal ideals (though they are), but because they limit the need for capital cities and corporates to fill the spaces in individuals' lives. Monopolistic or semi-monopolistic governance by its nature is slow, and the obvious port of call when there are problems. But its capacity to respond is slow and consistent with a broad-based model of support. Decentralised institutions of citizens and community are diverse and responsive, and able to address gaps that exit in the economy (through small businesses seeking out market opportunities) or civil governance (whether community groups or regional authorities) more swiftly and without the overheads that come from the operation of large systems.

In the end, Cameron's Big Society project failed, but not because a big society failed. It failed because a Big Society became about the devolution of government power, and therefore had fiscal ties to centralised government. A true Big Society is about decentralisation of political, social, cultural, and economic power that is proximate to individuals, not centralised government.

The idea of decentralisation as a political approach was advanced around the same time in Australia. Then Leader of the Opposition in New South Wales, Barry O'Farrell, spoke of the need for a "decade of decentralisation".[36] Little followed, and the reason is simple: to be a liberal involves ultimately wanting little power, and that rarely comes naturally to those who pursue the institutions of power. To understand the importance of decentralisaton for liberalism is to appreciate the inherent scepticism that should pertain to centralised power.

Central power depends on the strength of those it serves. A decentralised model of governance, society, and economy is one built upwards from the individual: the voter, the citizen, and the consumer. Graphically, it is like a pyramid. There may be strength at the top, but it always depends on the breadth and strength of its foundations. And the stronger the foundations, the more weight can be supported and the greater the structure that can be built. So too , in politics, the stronger the foundations of the political pyramid, the stronger the political apex, but proportionately the power rests with the many and the more their needs are met, the more readily the apex can preserve itself without disruption, and disempowerment of the many mean the top will ultimately fall.

A centralised model is built from the top downwards; from the strength of the capital, the bureaucrat, and the corporation down. Centralisation doesn't take the shape of an upside pyramid, but more like a game of Jenga. Jenga involves horizontal rectangular tiles in a column consisting of layers each having three tiles laid alongside one another in the same direction, and the next layer with the tiles arranged in the opposite direction, and this continues as high as the players can go. The game of Jenga is to remove a lower brick always to feed the top, until it ultimately topples. When power only rests at the top it inevitably feeds itself and can only do it through compromising the strength of its foundations. The greater the weight at the top, the more strength has been transferred from below. And since there will always be a few who benefit from disempowering others, the top will become heavier than its support. Hayek explained "why the worst get to the top":

> The totalitarian leader must collect around him a group which is prepared voluntarily to submit to that discipline they are to impose by force upon the rest of the people. That socialism can be put into practice only by methods of which most socialists disapprove is, of course, a lesson learned by many social reformers in the past . . . collectivism means the end of truth. To make a totalitarian system function efficiently it is not enough that everybody should be forced to work for the ends selected by those in control; it is essential that the people should come to regard these ends as their own.[37]

The more power is devolved, the harder it is for the central authority to hoover up the pickings, but the easier it is for individuals to access and earn them. Therefore, the only pathway to a truly liberal society is central leaders recognising that they aren't the solution to the problem, they are often the problem.

Conclusion

The new social contract

The Australian skepticism

Australians have always been skeptical of people who put ideas ahead of lived reality. It is a common saying to never trust a teetotaller. A wowser is someone who puts their personal puritanism ahead of the need of a crutch to manage the sobriety of life. In his history of reconstruction after the Second World War, the historian Stuart Macintyre recounts the story of the economist Lyndhurst Giblin explaining to a British audience the influence of his profession back home. Giblin explained that "in Australian usage the word 'academic' was a term of complaint or abuse".[1] And that has not changed much. In the 1990s, the prime minister, Paul Keating, made an art of framing the opposition leader, Dr John Hewson, with a simple derisory emphasis on his title to foster a belief of a disconnect between Hewson and his understanding of everyday Australian life.

Even today, the easiest dismissal of a good idea in a political debate is to simply label it as ideological and that it amounts to intellectual purity trumping reality.

So it is hardly surprising that Australians don't engage much with ideas like natural rights. They always have a preference for the 'she'll be right' attitude. Yet, ideas still matter. Political philosophies don't need a constituency. Their values and principles can exist without devotees. Many political ideologies lack broad-based support but persist because of the objectives they pursue. If you doubt that, just look at a Senate ballot paper at the next election. But if they want to turn ideology into outcomes, it needs a supportive constituency in a democracy: a political party (or parties) that wants to advance its aims and voters who share the benefits. It is easy to corral political movements around individual objectives amongst those who will benefit from them. The relationship between support and benefit is explicit. Ironically, liberalism is the reverse. Its beneficiaries are individuals, but the relationship between its principles and how people benefit is indirect and depends on an earned livelihood. It therefore has to live in each person's heart and mind against the temptation of short cuts to utopia.

Ideas have shaped the debates that have defined our country. But it is their pragmatic, non-ideological implementation that is the foundation of the Australian social contract to build a country for individuals to live their best lives. The life of the early colonies was full of debate about the structure of a new society that would enable individuals to pursue their own dreams. Physically removed from the traditions and structures they left behind, an unconstrained spirit gave the settlers a freedom to design new communities and colonies that would later become a country. Federation distilled these ideas into a document as a practical instrument to form government. The post-Federation Australian settlement focused on how to build that nation, based on the idea that incomes for individuals should be prioritised through industrial development. The post-War Menzies era focused on broadening the development of industry for jobs, to ensure individuals could secure homes so that the 'little platoons' could become 'little capitalists'. The neo-liberal era of equity extraction recognised the need to rebalance the inefficiencies of the post-War era and make Australia competitive against the backdrop of a changing world in order to sustain incomes.

The Australian promise

The concepts of the social contract and political ideology are esoteric to many Australians, but the idea of 'the great Australian dream' is not. It is not a contract created for unbridled freedom to be left alone, but the freedom to earn a livelihood and take responsibility. The promise of Australia has been for individuals to live life well. And the trade-off is that if you got this chance, then you were happy for everyone else to get it too. And living life well involves individuals living across the full spectrum of life and freely moving through the stages from opportunity to security limited only by their own effort. Living life well involves equality of *opportunity* for every individual to get a good start through a decent education, a chance at a job with a decent income, and then enjoying the *security* of a family home before retiring with dignity. And while liberalism speaks to all of these stages, the data shows its electoral appeal depends on whether individuals graduate out of merely seeking opportunity, and earn a living sufficient to accumulate something worth protecting, notably the purchase of a home. Once they do, they are electorally less interested in ideologies that promote the idea of opportunity and refocus to those interested in conserving the status quo.

For the most part, Australia has been able to deliver on this promise. Not everyone has started in the same position. People can come from moneyed families, but the structures and systems don't unduly favour them socially or economically. One of the most important underpinnings of the contract has been that it has been democratic. Since the arrival of Europeans, the objective has been to develop Australia as a liberal country. Large landholdings (at least compared with the size of the continent) were never allocated to create a new hereditary nobility. The call for a bunyip aristocracy of hereditary peerage and land received derision in the mid-nineteenth century, and recent evidence about attempts to reinstate the title of knights and dames suggests things haven't changed much. It is because, as a liberal nation, we understand that individuals are expected to earn their reward, not inherit it or have it bestowed on them. As prices rise, younger generations are becoming dependent on their parents to buy their own home. We should not want the only pathway for a younger generation to buy their own home to be dependent on the financial means of their parents; particularly when most Australians both grow their wealth, and hold it, in their own home. It risks creating a neo-aristocracy. And more importantly, we shouldn't tolerate generations being locked out of the housing market because of the decisions of their parents. That would undermine liberal meritocracy and social mobility.

The Australian problem

If liberalism is to continue delivering, it must recalibrate. Freedom of the individual matters, but one principle does not make the full meal of an ideology alone. The era of equity extraction sought to redress the inefficiencies of flawed decision-making. But it didn't just extract economic capital. It extracted capital in non-economic institutions as well. And while it delivered economic prosperity, it has also enabled the bureaucratisation of many aspects of civil society. It has tied too many of the structures of society to central government, instead of attaching them to the wellspring of individuals voluntarily collaborating to address shared aims and improve our social fabric.

To redress the imbalance, liberalism must reacquaint itself with its own tradition of justice. There is a rich vein to draw from. Liberals have often been at the forefront of formulating concepts of justice, particularly equality of opportunity. But equality of opportunity is not just based on access to elementary education. It is to live in an open society that creates no artificial barriers that inhibit any individual's capacity to succeed. It is on this basis that liberals must reject prejudice. It's why protectionism and anti-competitive regulation is illiberal. Under the false banner of helping jobs, it only works to serve established interests. It is also why intergenerational justice has a place. Its place is not one of the blind pursuit of equity or equality of outcome. It is a liberal conviction that each generation should have the equality of opportunity to earn their own livelihood. It is an intergenerational justice that does not create preferences for established generations any more than it punishes those having 'a go'. It is why liberals rightly oppose intergenerational debt. It is why liberals are committed to environmental stewardship. And it is why liberals should believe that each generation should take responsibility for themselves, and not burden those who follow them with the costs of the earlier generation's choices.

The demographic challenge

The ageing demographic challenge is real. Societies have never been blessed with as many retired people. Our ability to keep people alive and provide them with a high quality of life is the compounded benefits of human progress in many areas of endeavour from sanitation to healthcare systems, scientific research and economic growth. We have also never had so many retired people, as well as so many young people at the same time. And that creates its own unique dynamic—when one generation is so desperately seeking opportunity and the other security.

Older Australians have had their chance to succeed, and they should want every individual in every generation that follows to have that same freedom to live their best lives too. Throughout the Covid-19 pandemic, the young have been prepared to compassionately sacrifice their interests to contain a crisis that disproportionately affects the elderly. That sacrifice is real in their education, their incomes, and their career progression. In the coming years, we shall all need to confront the economic cost of a health crisis that will disproportionately burden the next generation. That imbalance already existed. The pandemic has just made it more extreme.

Both tax and spending are a critical part of this discussion. Older Australians have already paid a working life of tax and that should be respected. A sustainable tax system is not one that is only paid at the income stage of life, but across the whole lifecycle. If people aren't carrying their equal share of the tax burden, it disconnects them from the contribution to a system from which they derive benefits and pushes the cost onto others. Only economists care about the consequences of tax rates they don't have to pay. And if you don't have to pay for access to services, you'll hardly want to ration access.

There is no fixed time period for contributing to the tax system. It is not just the responsibility of the young. One of the great problems of removing low income earners from the income tax system is they no longer care what the rate is. These principles don't change for any other section of society. A liberal society depends on people having a stake, and for structures to be open that don't create artificial constraints on individuals as they advance through their stages of life. It is why consumption-based taxation is the correct method for taxation; not profit taxes on individuals or companies. Consumption taxes aren't just paid by everyone today, they are paid at every stage of life. They give everyone a stake in the responsibility to carry the costs of the country.

Unless we accept the need for consumption taxes, the cost of supporting the elderly can only be passed on in one direction: toward younger people who have yet to have their go. And as David Willets explains, our current arrangement reverses the traditional downstream flow of the river. Traditionally, familial arrangements ensure support goes from established generations to younger ones to give them their shot at life. That can't be done if they're carrying the cost of themselves, their families, their own generation, and generations that preceded them too.

It would be wrongheaded for those who currently enjoy the benefits of this structural imbalance to think they have no interest in reform. It is quite the opposite. For decades, the Baby Boomers have been numerically supreme. That has now ended and the Millennials are numerically ascendant. At this stage of their life, Millenials have a natural interest in opportunity, while Baby Boomers have the same interest in security. It is why Baby Boomers should lead the dialogue about how to get it right and not allow it to fuel a culture of envy and resentment that is already bubbling under the surface. And, frankly, liberals should be more willing to embrace it, because the solutions to these problems are liberal ideas put into practice.

Empower individuals and decentalise power

So what should liberals do? First, empowerment is achieved through the freedom of individuals to choose and take responsibility. That can't happen when choices are made for people, or solutions imposed on them. There is a desperate need to reverse the trend of power and responsibility away from Canberra and corporates and back to communities and individuals. When relationships are bureaucratised, organic bonds are displaced. The foundations of modern Australia were based on a basic understanding that the strength of the country came from the empowerment of individuals, who formed families and communities as the bond of social solidarity. Empowerment necessitates people being able to live the full expression of their life, and that can't be done in isolation. As Adam Smith understood, much of life is found in mutualism. It is one of the oddities of people's misunderstanding of liberalism—that it breeds selfishness. It is quite the reverse. Liberalism breeds self-reliance and responsibility, and it fosters voluntary cooperation in community and commerce. The most selfish act that anyone can indulge in is to choose not to stand on their own two feet, because it necessarily passes the burden on to others to provide support. And not only does that individual then burden another, they're consuming the same energy that could be used to support others who cannot stand up themselves. Needless dependence is selfishness. And the greatest demonstration of selfishness is people clawing to get their equal share of the socialist system they believe they contribute to.

Every time power is removed from individuals, it gravitates to central authority. Until the trend toward centralism ends, there will be dissatisfaction over our democracy. Populism arises from unaccountability and a weakening of the causal relationship between democratic action and outcomes. These problems will only be addressed by closing the feedback loops between people and outcomes. We need to address the proximity gap between individuals and their capacity to effect change. The constant push for streamlined governance under the banner of efficiency is a recipe for government by monopoly. We don't like monopolies in any other aspect of the country. In business, we understand monopolies are predatory and exploitative against the individual. So why would anything be different in governance? Monopolising unitary government is not just a bad idea, it is dangerous.

The Australian federation is an incredible expression of liberalism. It reflects the basic objective of subsidiarity that laws and programmes should be designed, developed, and implemented closest to the people they affect because it leads to better outcomes and higher accountability, and addresses declining levels of trust. Liberals should defend it vigorously, and they should develop a plan to aggressively reassert it at the heart of Australia's democracy—particularly through fiscal decentralisation, so that those that spend are also compelled to tax and take responsibility for both sides of their ledger.

Reasserting the federation is a beginning. David Cameron's Big Society project was a British solution to a British problem, but the spirit and focus of it is fundamentally correct. Australia has always been fortunate that it hasn't crowded out private providers from the public square too much. Unlike the secularism enforced in some other countries, we haven't prohibited civil society from providing services and offering individuals alternatives to government programmes, such as health or education. There should be more of it and across the board. The role of government is to address issues of inequity. This means ensuring access to the things we deem essential for equality of opportunity. But it is better to break up equity funding and service delivery to drive competition and innovation. It should not be an exercise in outsourcing government service provision. It should be an exercise in empowerment, in which individuals are free to choose and take responsibility. Milton Friedman wrote extensively of the need to do so in education through a voucher system. But the same principles apply in terms of what and how we subsidise when it comes to healthcare. It is also true of schemes for public insurances of life, like unemployment benefits, as well as the private insurance through superannuation.

Such an endeavour is not for the faint hearted. It depends on the need to rebalance the understanding of people's own relationship to risk and responsibility. And it also requires government understanding that although it has a role, it isn't the solution to all of society's ills. It is not impossible. Clients of the National Disability Insurance Scheme are given significantly more control over choices for service provision than most people who access services at a local public hospital.

Prioritise homeownership

Secondly, we need to look at homeownership as central to public policy. Homeownership is the greatest manifestation of individuals' opportunity to pursue their own security. It necessarily depends on work, discipline, and reward for sacrifice. For liberalism, it is the conversion point that leads generations to have a stake in their country and align their interests to the conservation of the status quo and the advancement of the country's interests.

Over the past thirty years, the only age demographic that has seen a rise in homeownership is Australians over 65, and that's only in the top income quintile. Homeownership is now projected to be so scarce that, by 2040, only half of Australians between 25 and 55 will own their own home.[2] The follow through is an increasing number of people entering retirement without the security of a home. That will have very real consequences for liberalism's political constituency—and it won't be good. The less people have an interest in the status quo, the less they will be interested in conserving it.

That doesn't mean policy around housing should be taken from the States and given to Canberra. Quite the reverse—if you really want to destroy the development of housing policy, then centralise it. What it does mean is that it needs to be factored into State and federal policymaking a lot more. Housing has an economic value. But it shouldn't be treated solely as a wealth storing vehicle: it must be treated for what it is: the foundation of people's security and safety. The more we increase homeownership rates, the stronger the foundations for individuals will be, and therefrom flows the strength of the nation. But people can only do so if housing is affordable.

Homeownership is fundamentally about supply and demand.

And demand has continued to grow aided by immigration. Supply, and particularly affordable supply, has been constrained by a host of factors. They range from land release policies of State governments, which rely on it for revenue through both sale and transaction taxes, to planning regulations that empower people to stop increasing the volume of available stock, environmental regulations designed to make housing more sustainable over the long run, but which carry higher upfront costs, cheap debt that encourages greater borrowing, and an imbalanced tax system. There are more, but each one depends on a degree of balance. Everyone accepts that some degree of planning is necessary in established areas. But I'll never forget a conversation with a resident while doorknocking in the affluent Melbourne suburb of Jolimont for a local council election campaign. Ready to make the case for my candidature, I walked up the path to the beautifully presented white terrace house with rose bush gardens. Listening to their concerns, I was struck by the complete dissonance produced by their biggest complaint about the inability of the children to buy a home nearby and their staunch opposition to any new housing development. Obviously, people can't have it all and need to be involved in the process of assessing trade-offs in any discussion about planning. That won't change. It has to be a constant and evolving discussion. But it is one that should be better informed, and frankly clearer. There should be democratic accountability over planning development, but that does not mean monopoly. People should be able to buy land with a clear understanding of the parameters of what can be done with it. There should be clear boundaries for developers who adhere to guidelines with complementary fast tracking for planning approvals to minimise landholding and financing costs. Waiting a year or longer for planning approval is unnecessary and the cost is only borne by the purchaser. It isn't the only trade off we need to confront. We need to have a proper discussion about height limits and what it means for the communities we are creating, because enforcing low density in some communities necessitates higher density elsewhere. And when it comes to the livability of a community, both lead to islands. It is only a question of whether they are horizontal in low-density urban sprawl or vertical high-density towers; whereas medium density can build community.

What we have to do is to allow Australians to get their priorities right. At the moment, we compel people to start saving for their retirement security when they are still in the opportunity stage of their life. Compulsory superannuation is forgone wages. Compelling people to save for up to fifty years into the future while they can't afford homeownership today is patently absurd. It is the asset that is hardest to secure, and the one in which Australians hold most of their wealth. And if people haven't paid off their home at retirement, the first thing they do is dip into their superannuation to pay it off. But that assumes retirees have a home. One of the most disturbing trends has been the rise of single women retiring without superannuation or a property. It is essentially a life at risk of finishing in poverty.

No one disputes the compounded benefit of saving for retirement early. But the compounded benefit from homeownership is much greater for the individual and the country. It is more rational to assess how the financial equity in an owner-occupied home can be extracted as part of retirement, than to delay homeownership today so people can start saving for their distant retirement. Forced savings for future retirement security shouldn't become the tradeoff for the opportunity of the great Australian dream.

An intergenerational tax system

Thirdly, we also need to ensure intergenerational justice is considered in the tax system by simplifying taxes, applying them more broadly, and reducing concessions as a trade-off for lower and more consistent rates. House prices are affected by supply and demand, but the tax system unnecessarily encourages ownership as an asset not to be traded. The real issue is not treating losses on property differently from other forms of income, it is the income, capital gain, and transaction costs on property that entrench interests. The real damage is done by stamp duty. People move through stages of life, and their housing reflects those stages. Many young Australians know the moment that they put the 'SOLD' sticker across the sale board of their first one or two-bedroom apartment. And it doesn't take long before they're upgrading because of changing circumstances, normally because they've entered into a relationship, got married, or had kids—or the kids are getting older. Unsurprisingly, as the family grows, so does the space required. But that only lasts so long, and, as we age and the kids move out, our need for a large home goes with it. It's time to downsize. States now waive stamp duty on a first purchase because of the prohibitive barrier it creates for Australians saving a deposit. Yet, through stamp duty, the tax system discourages Australians from trading their housing and acquiring a property that reflects their current stage of life. Every day, stamp duty leads people to stay in their existing home longer and slows the movement of others and increases prices. It also encourages the retention of housing as an investment.

Inconsistent tax rates make the problem worse and encourage people to structure their financial arrangements so as to attract the lowest rate.[4] But it isn't just how taxes impact on housing. The other problem is the high differential tax rates that apply on the primary way young people get ahead—income. While capital gains from appreciation of holding assets is taxed at half the applied rate, effectively entrenching the benefit of having and holding assets which can only exist if you're established. There's no intergenerational justice in such preferential arrangements and it means those seeking opportunity have to carry a higher share of the burden in direct tax today, or future repayments on debt tomorrow.

These are not easy problems to solve. Their solution depends on framing the nature of the challenge properly. At the 2019 federal election, the Labor Party got that discussion very, very wrong. Their malicious campaign against recipients of refundable franking credits,[5] which they considered a taxpayer-funded gift, demonized older Australians who had structured their finances to enable them to be independent and secure in retirement.[6]

Successful reform depends on getting the conversation right. There are a lot of good arguments for wholesale tax reform. If you ask many economists, they'll talk of the need to make the system more efficient. It's about the least persuasive argument that can be made—a dry rationale for a dry topic. It isn't just because it equates to dollars and cents. It is because it lacks humanity and carries no moral weight. When John Howard and Peter Costello argued for a goods and services tax, they highlighted the absurdity of private jets not attracting sales tax while ordinary consumer products did. A just political system has to treat people fairly.

The objective of tax reform should be focused on how it empowers individuals to live their fullest lives and buy their own homes while sharing responsibility for society. The tax system must have intergenerational justice at its core. It must seek to harmonise tax rates that are as low, as broad, and as consistent as possible. This will remove the incentive for established interests to structure their finances so as to reduce their tax obligations to the detriment of the next generation.

The post-pandemic social contract

In the Introduction, I cautioned that the trends outlined in these pages risked a soft revolution if there wasn't an evolution. Australians aren't much for pitch forks and burning barns. The trends existed before the Covid-19 pandemic. An article by Richard Hass in *Foreign Affairs* argues that "the world following the pandemic is unlikely to be radically different from the one that proceeded it", and it "will not so much change the basic direction of world history as accelerate it."[3] Of course, the pandemic has raised a whole series of other problems that will cascade for years to come, particularly the impact on employment and the collapse of businesses, as well as the realignment of geopolitical relations. But the testing of the social contract existed before the pandemic. The pressure on it will only be exacerbated. While housing will no doubt drop in price, so will incomes and the number of people who are employed. People won't be locked out of home ownership because of prices, but because of their incapacity to save or have basic economic security.

The pandemic will only highlight the problems outlined in this book and bring forward the need for reform. Young people who have had their economic interests sacrificed to address the health crisis will want their go too. And they should want their chance to live their fullest life. The task for liberals is to see the moment for the opportunity that the crisis provides. The opportunity is to correct a liberalism that became imbalanced over the past thirty years and get a liberalism focused on empowering individuals back on track and appealing again. The social contract depends on focusing on how our society and economy can empower individuals by focusing on and home ownership, not by narrowly pursuing just their freedom. If liberals renew the social contract in this way, it will provide the ingredients to entrench liberalism into the psyche of a new generation and secure future chapters of the continuing Australian liberal story.

Notes

1. The evolution of empowerment

1   E. Fawcett, *Liberalism: The Life of an Idea* (Princeton University Press, 2018), p. 1.

2   A. Ryan. *The Making of Modern Liberalism* (Princeton University Press, 2012), p. 1.

3   *Ibid.*

4   *Ibid.*, p. 24.

5   *Ibid.*, p. 25.

6   J. Lonsdale, "Libertarianism is Dysfunctional, but Liberty is Great", The Mont Pelerin Society 1980-2020, 2020, p. 3.

7   L. Siedentop, *Inventing the Individual: The Origins of Western Liberalism* (Harvard University Press, 2014), p. 28.

8   *Ibid.*, p. 77.

9   *Ibid.*, p. 173.

10 *Ibid.*, p. 158.

11 *Ibid.*, p. 217.

12 *Ibid.*, pp. 243-244.

13 D. Hannan, *How We Invented Freedom and Why It Matters* (Head of Zeus, 2015), p. 110.

14 Bagehot, "Some thoughts on the crisis of liberalism—and how to fix it", *The Economist*, 12 June 2018.

2. Australian liberalism

1   D. Kemp, *The Land of Dreams: How Australians won their freedom 1788-1860* (Miegunyah Press, 2019), Vol. 1, Kindle location 188.

2   T. Lynch, "Australian liberalism old and new", *The Conversation*, 1 July 2013.

3   A. A. Staley and J. R. Nethercote, *Liberalism and the Australian Federation* (Federation Press, 2001), p. 23.

4   R. G. Menzies, Address at the Federal Council of the Liberal Party of Australia, Canberra, 6 April 1964.

5   H. Collins, *Political Ideology in Australia: The Distinctiveness of a Benthamite Society*, (MIT Press, 1985), p. 151.

6   C. Kukathas, *Liberalism: The International Context* (Federation Press, 2011), p. 25.

7   Kemp, Kindle location 485.

8   H. Collins, *Political Ideology in Australia: The Distinctiveness of a Benthamite Society*, p. 147.

9   *Ibid.*, p. 148.

10 *Ibid.*, p. 149.

11 New Zealand was the first country to give women the right to vote but it did not extend the franchise to standing for Parliament.

12 S. Macintyre, *Australia's Boldest Experiment: War and reconstruction in the 1940s* (NewSouth Books, 2015), p. 223.

13 T. Bramston, *Robert Menzies: The Art of Politics* (Scribe Publications, 2019), Kindle

location 5679.

14 *Ibid.*, Kindle location 1939.

15 R. G. Menzies, Address at a conference of anti-Labor political parties, Canberra, 13 October 1944.

16 R. G. Menzies, Speech following election victory, Melbourne, 10 November 1949.

17 R. G. Menzies, "The Forgotten People" radio broadcast, 22 May 1942.

18 A. Martin, *The 'Whig' View of Australian History and Other Essays* (Melbourne University Press, 2007), p. 245.

19 R. G. Menzies, Address to Newington College, Sydney, 29 April 1961.

20 R. G. Menzies, Address at Federal Council of the Liberal Party of Australia, Canberra, 6 April 1964.

21 R. G. Menzies, Policy speech at City Hall, Kew, 15 November 1961.

22 R. G. Menzies, Address to the International Congress on Human Relations, Melbourne, 3 May 1965.

23 The first two were focused on freedom of speech and expression, with the second more focused on freedom of the media.

24 I. Berlin, "Two concepts of liberty" in *Four Essays on Liberty* (Oxford University Press, 1969), p. 3.

25 R. G. Menzies, "Freedom from Want", Broadcast Radio 2UE, 10 July 1942.

26 Ibid.

27 R. G. Menzies, *Letters to My Daughter,* (Murdoch Books, 2011), Kindle location 4351.

28 Ibid., Kindle location 4424.

29 See: <https://electionspeeches.moadoph.gov.au/explore>.

30 R. G. Menzies, Address to the Federal Council of the Liberal Party of Australia, Canberra, 12 April 1965.

31 R. G. Menzies, Address at the W.A. Convention of the Liberal Party, South Perth, 30 July 1962.

32 R. G. Menzies, Address at the International Congress on Human Relations, Melbourne, 3 May 1965.

33 R. G. Menzies, Jefferson Oration, Virginia, 4 July 1963.

34 R. G. Menzies, Address to opening of Liberal Party Headquarters, Canberra, 9 November 1965.

35 R. G. Menzies, Address to Exhibition of Australian Art, Adelaide, 17 March 1962.

36 R. G. Menzies, Address to Young Liberal Movement Convention, Sydney, 27 July 1962.

37 R. G. Menzies, Speech at lunchtime rally, Sydney, 5 April 1965.

38 A. Reid, "The Age of Menzies", *The Bulletin*, 29 January 1966, p. 10.

39 Bramston, p. 101.

40 *Ibid.*, p. 314.

41 R. G. Menzies, The First William Queale Memorial Lecture, Adelaide, 22 October 1954.

42 R. G. Menzies, Election speech, Camberwell, 10 August 1946.

43 R. G. Menzies, "The Forgotten People".

3. The neo-liberal era of equity

1   K. Rudd, "The global financial crisis", *The Monthly*, February 2009.

2   D. Yergin and J. Stanislaw, *The Commanding Heights: The Battle for the World Economy* (Free Press, 2002), pp. 110-111.

3   M. Rosner, "The short history of global living conditions and why it matters that we know it", Our World in Data.

4   See: <https://populationmatters.org/the-facts/resources-consumption>.

5   D. Stern, "The Rise and Fall of the Environmental Kuznets Curve", *World Development,* Vol. 32, Issue 8.

6   C. Mims, "A Surprisingly Long List of Everything Smartphones Replaced", *MIT Technology Review*, 23 July 2012.

7   A. McAfee, *"More From Less": The surprising story of how we learned to prosper using fewer resources – and what happens next* (Simon & Schuster, 2019), p. 4.

8   *Ibid.*, p. 100.

9   *Ibid.*, p. 238.

10 S. Cameron and I. McAllister, "The 2019 Australian Federal Election Study", ANU School of Politics and International Relations.

11 P. Mair, *Ruling the Void: The hollowing of Western Democracy* (Verso, 2013), p. 84.

12 G. Stoker, M. Evans and M. Halupka, *Trust and Democracy in Australia: Democratic decline and renewal* (Democracy 2025, 2018), p. 26.

13 Edelman Trust Barometer, Global Report, 2019.

14 China is ranked 87 of 180 countries, United Arab Emirates is 23 out of 180 countries, Indonesia, 89 out of 180 countries, and India, 78 out of 180 countries.

15 E. Ortiz-Ospina and M. Roser, "Trust", Our World in Data.

16 R. Willingham and J. Dunstan, "Extreme heat due to climate change could send cricket's Boxing Day Test into extinction, researchers say", ABC, 27 December 2019.

17 B. Chappell, "Beer Prices Could Double Because Of Climate Change, Study Says", NPR, 16 October 2018.

18 L. Barber, H. Foy and A. Barker, "Vladimir Putin says liberalism has 'become obsolete", *Financial Times,* 28 June 2019.

19 See: <https://www.slv.vic.gov.au/contribute-create/vicfix/eight-hours-movement>.

20 H. Collins, *Political Ideology in Australia: The Distinctiveness of a Benthamite Society,* (MIT Press, 1985), p. 149.

21 Kemp, Kindle location 1154.

22 *Ibid.*, p. 290.

23 See: <http://oll-resources.s3.amazonaws.com/titles/101/0199_Bk.pdf>.

24 *Ibid.*

25 Year Book Australia 1909, p. 263,

26 *Ibid.*

27 *Ibid.*

28 Kemp, Kindle location 1240.

29 *Ibid.*, Kindle location 9513.

30 P. Kelly, *The End of Certainty*, (Allen & Unwin, 2008), pp. 1-2.

31 R.G. Menzies, *The Measure of the Years* (Cassell, 1970), p. 55.

32 A. Smith, *The Theory of Moral Sentiments* (1759), Kindle location 1290.

33   *Ibid.*, p. 139.

34   *Ibid.*, p. 147.

35   E. Burke, Reflections on the Revolution in France (1790).

36   F. A. Hayek, *Law, Legislation and Liberty: A new statement of the liberal principles of justice and political economy*, (Taylor & Francis, 2012), p. 295.

37   M. Friedman, *Free to Choose: A personal statement* (Cengage Learning EMEA, 1990), p. 132.

38   K. Popper, *The Open Society and Its Enemies* (Routledge, 1994), p. 165.

39   F. A. Hayek, *The Road to Serfdom* (University of Chicago Press, 1944), p. 57.

40   J. Rawls, *A Theory of Justice* (Harvard University Press, 1971), p. 290.

41   *Ibid.*, p. 288.

4. Liberalism's social licence

1   S. Roberts, "Washington Talk: Reagan and the Russians – The Joke's on Them", *The New York Times*, 21 August 1987.

2   F. A. Hayek, *The Road to Serfdom*, (1944), p59.

3   W. Vamplew (ed.), *Australian Historical Statistics*, 1976 to 1993: ABS, Trade Union Members, cat. no. 6325.0; 1994 to 2013: ABS, Employee Earnings Benefits and Trade Union Membership, cat. no. 6310.0; 2014 to 2018: ABS, Characteristics of Employment, cat. no. 6333.0.

4   *Ibid.*

5   Electricity, gas, waste, and water.

6   ABS, Employee Earnings Benefits and Trade Union Membership.

7   Around two million according to the Australian Bureau of Statistics.

8   Public arguably also includes those who predominantly live off taxpayer-funded welfare.

9   C. Murray, *Coming Apart: The State of White America 1960-2010* (Crown Forum, 2013), p. 17.

10   *Ibid.*, p. 18.

11   *Ibid.*, p. 21.

12   I completed the survey and did pretty well.

13   Murray, p. 125.

14   *Ibid.*, p. 182.

15   *Ibid.*, p. 207.

16   *Ibid.*, p. 234.

17   J. D. Vance, *Hillbilly Elegy: A Memoir of a Family and Culture in Crisis*, (HarperCollins, 2016), p. 249.

18   *Ibid.*, p. 251.

19   D. Goodhart, *The Road to Somewhere: The New Tribes Shaping British Politics* (Penguin, 2017), p. 10.

20   *Ibid.*, p. 11.

21   Ironically, at the time the Secretary of State for Foreign and Commonwealth Affairs was the current Prime Minister, Boris Johnson.

22   Though slow wage growth is progressively fuelling some resentment, and a significant economic downturn could bring such a resentment forward.

23 M. Lesh, *Democracy in a Divided Australia* (Connor Court, 2018), p. 12.

24 *Ibid.*, p. 25.

25 That he describes as "highly educated Greens, inner-city progressive Labor".

26 That he describes as "working class traditional Labor".

27 Inner-city middle class "Turnbull" Liberals.

28 Lesh, p. 37.

5. Generation confrontation

1 G. Banks, *Health costs and policy in an Ageing Australia*, (Productivity Commission, Commonwealth of Australia, 2008), p. 9.

2 R. Morton and R. Tanner, "Generation & bigger than boomers and Xers", *The Australian*, 1 July 2017.

3 While 36 to 55 age bracket is 26.09 per cent of the population, this broader age group is proportionately smaller when weighted against the breadth of the age grouping.

4 M. McCrindle, "The Generation Map" in *The ABC of XYZ*, (UNSW Press, 2012).

5 B. Salt, "Australia's great divide", *The Australian*, 14 February 2020.

6 K. Parker, "The Big Generation Gap at the Polls Is Echoed in Attitudes on Budget Tradeoffs", Pew Research Center, 20 December 2012.

7 "Baby Boomers: The Gloomiest Generation", Pew Research Center, 25 June 2008.

8 B. Stokes, "Millennials in many countries are more open than their elders on questions of national identity", Pew Research Center, 16 February 2017.

9 S. Hannan-Morrow and M. Roden, "Gender, Age and Generational Effects on Turnout in Australian Federal Elections", The Australian Political Studies Association Annual Conference (University of Sydney Paper, 2014), p. 14.

10 Ibid., p. 13.

11 1C. Curtis, "How Britain voted at the 2017 general election", YouGov, 14 June 2017.

12 C. Curtis, "The demographics dividing Britain", YouGov, 25 April 2017.

13 A. McDonnell and C. Curtis, "How Britain voted in the 2019 election", YouGov, 17 December 2019.

14 T. Helm and M. Savage, "Jolt for Tories as poll suggests under-45s switching to Labour", *The Guardian*, 1 October 2017.

15 *Ibid.*

16 "Exit polls", CNN (2016).

17 "The best electoral roll in history", Australian Electoral Commission, 23 April 2019, see: <https://www.aec.gov.au/media/media-releases/2019/04-23.htm>.

18 S. Wright and M. Koslowski, "Voter turnout at record low after young people disengage", *Sydney Morning Herald*, 31 May 2019.

19 P. Karp, "Women, young voters and inner-city dwellers drive survey enrolments", *The Guardian*, 2 October 2017.

20 S. Wright and M. Koslowski, *Sydney Morning Herald*.

21 J. Bullard, C Garriga and C. J. Waller, "Demographics, Redistribution and Optimal Inflation" in *Federal Reserve Bank of St. Louis Review*, 2012, Vol. 94, No. 6, p. 437.

6. Marrying your mortgage

1   S. Cameron and I. McAllister, "Trends in Australian Political Opinion", *Australian Election Study 1987-2019* (ANU, 2019), p. 82.

2   C. Tilford, "The millennial moment in charts", *Financial Times*, 6 June 2018.

3   V. Winter, "Exclusive: even baby boomers think baby boomers get the best deal from the government", *The Feed*, 16 May 2019.

4   K. Johnstone, "Boomers, your privileged, tax-deducted time is up: Millenials have arrived", *Sydney Morning Herald*, 16 November 2018.

5   J. Daley and D. Wood, "Malcolm Turnbull be warned: the young are coming", *The Guardian*, 26 June 2017.

6   D. Willetts, *The Pinch: How the Baby Boomers Took Their Children's Future – And Why They Shoud Give It Back* (Atlantic, 2011) p. 253.

7   *Ibid.*, p. 124

8   A. Lowrey, "The Great Affordability Crisis Breaking America", *The Atlantic*, 7 February 2020.

9   *Ibid.*

10 "Accessible Manifestos", UK Labour Party, see: <https://labour.org.uk/manifesto-2019/accessible-manifestos/>.

11 *Ibid.*

12 "Youth Manifesto", UK Labour Party, see: <https://labour.org.uk/wp-content/uploads/2019/11/Digital-Youth-Manifesto.pdf>.

13 "Bernie Sanders on the issues", Bernie Campaign, see: <https://berniesanders.com/issues/>.

14 *Ibid.*

15 "The Reason-Rupe Millenial Survey", Reason Foundation, 10 July 2014, p. 8.

16 *Ibid*, p. 92.

17 E. Burke, *Reflections on the Revolution in France* (1790), Kindle location 19385.

18 *Ibid.*, p. 83.

19 R. Pipes, *The Russian Revolution* (Vintage, 1991), p. 112.

20 R. G. Menzies, "Forgotten People" radio broadcast, 22 May 1942.

21 H. de Soto, *The Mystery of Capital: Why Capitalism Triumphs in the West and Fails Everywhere Else* (Basic Books, 2000), p. 221.

22 R. G. Menzies, Election victory speech, Melbourne, 10 November 1949.

7. Disposable income avocados

1   B. Salt, "Moralisers, we need you!', *The Australian*, 17 October 2016.

2   B. Salt, "Smashed avo: you got me wrong", *The Weekend Australian Magazine*, 20 October 2017.

3   *Ibid.*

4   "'Don't buy $19 smashed avocado': Melbourne property tycoon hammers millennials over spending habits", 9NEWS, 15 May 2017.

5   "Distributions of the Australian population who have travelled overseas in the past year" as of April 2016, by age, Statista, August 2016.

6   Affordable meant around $3,000, and the aspiration was they wouldn't be networked simply to establish local area networks to play Doom and Quake. I got a second-

hand hand-me-down DOS-based laptop from my grandfather that didn't have a battery pack.

7   "Housing affordability", Essential Report, see: <http://www.essentialvision.com. au/housing-affordability-2>.

8   Consumer Price Index, Australian Bureau of Statistics, see: <https://www.abs.gov. au/AUSSTATS/abs@.nsf/mf/6401.0?opendocument&ref=HPKI>.

9   K. Griffiths and D. Wood, "Australia is facing a real generation gap of the kind we can't possibly want", *The Conversation,* 19 August 2019.

10 "Tax and Transfer Incidence in Australia", Australian Government Productivity Commission, October 2015, p. 72.

11 *Ibid.*

12 A small number of retirees with superannuation balances in excess of $1.6 million at the date of their retirement pay a concessional 15% tax rate on income derived from capital in excess of $1,600,000 held at the date of retirement.

13 "Tax and Transfer Incidence in Australia", p. 72.

14 See: <https://www.abc.net.au/news/2019-08-18/contributions/11425466>.

15 J. Sloan, "Let's not fall for this myth of generational injustice", *The Australian,* 25 June 2019.

16 D. Willetts, *The Pinch: How the Baby Boomers Stole Their Children's Future – And Why They Should Give It Back* (Atlantic Books, 2019), p. 258.

17 R. Fox and R. Finlay, "Dwelling prices and household income", Bulletin (Reserve Bank of Australia), December Quarter 2012.

18 T. Burke, C. Nyagaard and L. Ralston, "Australian home ownership: past reflections, future directions", AHURI Final Report, May 2020, p. 32.

19 *Ibid.*

20 *Ibid.,* p. 33.

21 R. Wilkins, P. Butterworth and E. Vera-Toscano, "The Household, Income and Labour Dynamics in Australia Survey: Selected Findings from Waves 1 to 17" (Melbourne Institute of Applied Economic and Social Research, 2017), p. 90.

22 Defined as those who did not own a home four years prior to the survey data.

23 Author's calculations based on HILDA data as cited by R. Wilkins, P. Butterworth and E. Vera-Toscano, p. 94.

24 D. Miles and J. Sefton, "Houses across time and across place", CEPR Discussion Paper, No. DP12103, 2017, pp. 45-46.

25 W. Fischel, *The Homevoter Hypothesis: How Home Values Influence Local Government Taxation, School Finance and Land-Use Policies* (Harvard University Press, 2001), p. 260.

26 D. Adler and B. Ansell, "Housing and populism", *West European Politics,* 2020, Vol. 43(2), pp. 344-365.

27 *Ibid.*

28 *Ibid.*

29 'First dimension' is a traditional left-right analysis of politics. 'Second dimension' politics is focused on 'insiders' versus 'outsiders' and comparable political analysis.

30 N. Ferguson and E. Freymann, "The Coming Generation War", *The Atlantic,* 6 May 2019.

31 S. Cameron and I. McAllister, "The 2019 Australian Federal Election – Results from the Australian Election Study" (ANU, 2019), p. 20.

32 The bottom ten electorates for marriage rates includes several Liberal electorates, most are atypical. Durack is the largest and one of the most decentrailsed electorates in Australia made up of remote mining communities in North-West Western Australia. So too is Leichhardt in Far North Queensland covering Cape York and Herbert anchored in Townsville with military installations, seasonal work and mining communities. Brisbane equally has an overall younger urban demographic like Sydney and Melbourne. The difference is Brisbane's geography and comparatively small size for a capital city includes many establishment suburbs that are in different electorates in Melbourne and Sydney, and that they are also anchored on the same side as the nearest water boundary—the Brisbane River. Almost all Liberal held seats are considered marginal electorates with lower primary votes. By comparison the Labor held seats have relatively high 2PP votes. By comparison the trend is much clearer for those electorates with the highest marital rates with almost all represented by Liberal MPs and with wide margins. All have primary votes above 50%, and in some cases 60%. There are two exceptions. Mayo in Southern South Australia is a traditionally held seat held by the Liberal Party that fell at the 2016 election as a result of a local MP that attracted notoriety and was beaten by a previous staff member who was subsequently re-elected as a popular independent. The other outlier is the Federal electorate of Greenway—a marginal swing electorate—that is a sliver of land between the electorate with the highest marriage rate—Mitchell in the North Western suburbs of Sydney—and Chifley in Western Sydney.

33 "The Genworth First Home Buyer Sentiment Report", Genworth, 2019, p. 6.

34 "The Bank Of Mum and Dad Goes Boom!", Digital Finance Analytics, 24 March 2019, see: <https://digitalfinanceanalytics.com/blog/tag/bank-of-mum-and-dad/>.

35 L. Ellis, "Opening Remarks to Plenary Panel at the Australasian Housing Researchers Conference", Reserve Bank of Australia, 16 February 2017.

36 G. Barrett, M. Cigdem, S. Whelan and G. Wood, "The relationship between intergenerational transfers, housing and economic outcomes", AHURI Final Report, October 2015, p. 64.

37 "Levels of household income and wealth", Australian Bureau of Statistics, 11/11/2019. see: https://www.abs.gov.au.

8. Big community, not Canberra

1 M. Nowak, UN Covenant on Civil and Political Rights CCPR Commentary, 2nd ed (N. P. Engel, 2005). P. 439.

2 F. A. Hayek, The Road to Serfdom (University of Chicago Press, 1994), p. 45.

3 Bagehot, "Some thoughts on the crisis of liberalism—and how to fix it", The Economist, 12 June 2018.

4 A. de Tocqueville, as cited in ibid.

5 Ibid.

6 Ibid.

7 OECD, "Making Decentralisation Work: A Handbook for Policy Makers", 2019, p. 16.

8 Ibid., p. 116.

9 S. J. Harper, Right Here, Right Now: Politics and Leadership in the Age of Disruption (Signal,

2019), p. 3.

10 *Ibid.*, p. 56.

11 *Ibid.*, p. 15.

12 *Ibid.*, p. 132.

13 *Ibid.*, p. 12.

14 W. Kristol, "Republican Donald Trump not the sort of president US conservatives want", *Financial Review,* 4 November 2016.

15 O. Haivry and Y. Hazony, "What is Conservatism?", *American Affairs,* 2017, Vol. 1(2).

16 *Ibid.*

17 *Ibid.*

18 A. Pabst, *The Demons of Liberal Democracy* (Polity Press, 2019), p. 2.

19 *Ibid.*, p. 5.

20 *Ibid.*, p. 121.

21 J. E. Ligthart and P. van Oudheusden, "In Government we trust: The role of fiscal decentralization", 2011, CentER Working Paper Series.

22 OECD, p. 117.

23 M. Tang and N. Huhe, "Does Decentralisation Bring the People Back to the Government? An Empirical Analysis of the Effect of Decentralisation on Political Trust", *Policy & Politics,* 2014, Vol. 37, p. 3.

24 D. Kemp, *The Land of Dreams: How Australians won their freedom 1788-1860* (Miegunyah Press, 2019), Vol. 1, Kindle location 492.

25 A. Smith, *Theory of Moral Sentiments* (1759), p. 139.

26 J. Norman, *Adam Smith: What He Thought, And Why It Matters* (Allen Lane, 2018), p. 51.

27 *Ibid.*, p. 53.

28 D. Kemp, *A Free Country: Australians' Search for Utopia 1861-1901* (Melbourne University Publishing, 2019), Vol. 2, Kindle location 10036.

29 R. G. Menzies, *Central Power in the Australian Commonwealth* (University Press of Virginia, 1967), p. 24.

30 *A Free Country,* Kindle location 10368.

31 A. Twomey and G. Withers, "Federalist Paper 1—Australia's Federal Future", Report for the Council for the Australian Federation, 2007, p. 4.

32 *Ibid.*, p. 5.

33 "They are casting their problems at society. And, you know, there's no such thing as society. There are individual men and women and there are families. And no government can do anything except through people, and people must look after themselves first. It is our duty to look after ourselves and then, also, to look after our neighbours.": M. Thatcher in "Margaret Thatcher: a life in quotes", *The Guardian,* 8 April 2013.

34 D. Cameron and N. Clegg, "The Coalition: Our Programme for government", 2010, p. 11.

35 D. Cameron, Address on Big Society, 10 Downing Street, London, 14 February 2011.

36 B. O'Farrell, Address to Shires Association of NSW 2010 Annual Conference, 1 June 2010.

37 F. A. Hayek, pp. 51 and 54.

Conclusion: The new social contract

1   S. Macintyre, *Australia's Boldest Experiment: War and reconstruction in the 1940s* (NewSouth Books, 2015), p. 73.

2   T. Burke, C. Nygaard and L. Ralston, *Australian home ownership: past reflections, future directions* (Australian Housing and Urban Research Institute, 2020), p. 1.

3   R. Hass, "The Pandemic will accelerate history rather than reshape it", *Foreign Affairs*, 7 April 2020.

4   When a top marginal income tax rate is in the high-40s, and company tax is trending to the mid-20s, only a fool would not seek to take advantage of the tax rate arbitrage. That's why people use trusts. When an investment property is held in a trust, it gains benefits. Even though there is a 50% discount on capital gains tax from the applied marginal rate, regardless of whether property is held by an individual or in a trust, the discrepancy in marginal income tax rates often makes a trust more attractive because of certainty and an often lower effective rate. It also delivers asset protection. If income tax rates were flatter and more consistent with company tax rates, there would be less of an incentive to use trusts, and to the extent they are used for asset protection reasons, the economic viability of insurance would become more attractive. It just creates headaches and generates billable hours for lawyers and accountants.

5   Refundable franking credits are tax offsets for company tax paid on shares. The tax offset is imputed through the dividend imputation system to an individual to stop them being double taxed. Those who have tax bills use to them to offset against their tax obligations. Those that don't get the company tax paid refunded.

6   Similarly, the Labor Party targeted those who had saved to purchase investment properties. And while the policy claimed to 'grandfather' existing owners—itself a serious issue, since the established were protected and the young denied protection—it too involved a failure to understand the problem. Negative gearing requires people to make forward investments and then lose money to provide additional housing. In practice, it suppresses prices for renters who are the people most likely to be saving for a first home. To scrap it amounts to taxing losses—a completely illogical thing to do. The reckless and tardy approach they took was exemplified by an older man at a local polling booth who said, "I've worked too hard to have them take it all away." Labor demonstrated how to have this conversation poorly.

Index